MICHAIL ANTONIO
HUMANS NOT ROBOTS

WHEN ELITE SPORT AND REAL LIFE COLLIDE

HarperCollins*Publishers*

HarperCollins*Publishers*
1 London Bridge Street
London SE1 9GF

www.harpercollins.co.uk

HarperCollins*Publishers*
Macken House, 39/40 Mayor Street Upper
Dublin 1, D01 C9W8, Ireland

First published by HarperCollins*Publishers* 2026

1 3 5 7 9 10 8 6 4 2

Photograph on dedication page courtesy of the author

A catalogue record of this book is
available from the British Library

ISBN 978-0-00-879723-2

Printed and bound in the UK using 100%
renewable electricity at CPI Group (UK) Ltd

CONTENTS

For my children:
Mikey, Miles, Myla, Mylo,
Sky, Saint and Star

PROLOGUE

Right there in front of me is the crumpled wreck of the Ferrari.

'I can't believe you're alive,' the guy at the compound tells me. 'I've seen vehicles with much less damage that people haven't come out of.'

It's taken a bit of willpower to get myself down here, to come face-to-face with a car which very nearly became a coffin. My eyes well up but the tears don't fall. I don't like to cry around people. It's something I've been working on with my therapist. She keeps telling me, 'Just let your emotions go!' But I've always buried them.

The tangle of metal and wire makes me realise just how close I came to dying. I've viewed the photos of the crash scene, but seeing the battered shell of the car there, and thinking how I was inside it, is so much worse. I feel my stomach turn over. The thought that I might not have been here to see my kids grow up jabs at the front of my mind.

My older brother Duke has driven me over here and he's trying to speak to me. But I need my own moment. I should really have come alone so I can take it all in. Slowly I walk round the car. In the background I hear: 'How did you get out of that?' A great question, and one I've been asked hundreds of times since pictures of the crash scene first appeared online. I always say the same thing: 'The bulk of my leg is probably what saved me.' That footballer's leg, toughened by years at the top of the game, was strong enough to absorb the majority of the impact. Had that not been the case it would have snapped, the artery would have broken, and, so I've been told, I'd have bled out within four minutes. Bearing in mind it took three-quarters of an hour to get me out of the vehicle, you don't have to be a genius to see how the drama would have ended. It's not something I want to dwell on, a reminder that while I have, to a certain degree, processed the accident, the trauma will last a long, long time.

As I walk away from the compound, I can't help thinking that, in some ways, the accident has come to define me. I'm no longer Michail Antonio the Premier League striker; I'm Michail Antonio the Premier League striker who survived a terrible car crash. I'd rather that wasn't the case, but at the same time I'm aware that what happened has allowed me to see the very best of humanity. There's something very powerful about knowing there are people out there who helped save your life. Not just the paramedics. There was the dog walker who first got to me, the man who called the ambulance, others who pulled up in the hope they could in some way come to my aid. Thinking of all those remarkable people has allowed me to see the more positive and human side of something awful.

It reminds me that I'm human too. Make no mistake, being a footballer is a role that can very easily take over your life. It shapes the person you are – how you see yourself and the world. In many ways, the moment you sign your first contract is the moment you leave reality behind. In its place comes an unstable existence of incredible highs and crushing lows. All played out to an ever-changing backdrop of players, managers and fans. From the outside, everyone thinks you've entered a gilded palace. And they're right. Trouble is it's built on quicksand.

In this weird environment, things that would be seen as outlandish, totally insane even, in any other field of life are thought entirely normal. Imagine if every time you walked into your office a load of people started bellowing abuse and making obscene hand gestures. That's extreme, right? But in football that sort of behaviour is dismissed as 'just the way it is'. Same with transfers. When was the last time you went on holiday for a fortnight and every time you opened the newspaper there was a story saying your employer was desperate to get rid of you? And yet stuff like that happens in football all the time. It's seen simply as part and parcel of the sport.

There's so much about being a footballer that's totally mad, and yet you're supposed to just roll with it, take it as it comes. I expect most people think we're all immune to the craziness, that we run on automatic. Machines detached from normal human emotion. It's something I found myself reflecting on a lot during my recovery, and, as my shattered leg healed, I started to think about explaining my thoughts in more detail. How it's about time a player told it how it *really* is. What it truly feels like to earn a living from playing professional football, day in, day out, season after season. I don't mean that in a moany way. Believe me, I've had plenty – PLENTY – of fun along the way. I mean in the most open and honest way possible, from someone who's seen the game from every possible angle, from the lower reaches of the pyramid to the top and everywhere in between.

I want to take you on that journey and show you how being a footballer is the greatest job on Earth. Why it's everything you probably think it is, and more. Let me be your guide and take you behind the scenes of this crazy game we call football. I'm under no illusion about how fortunate I am, and I would never want to disrespect the many that have a much tougher job than I ever will. But I also want to reveal how those lucky enough to be living this dream are, beneath the glitz and the glamour, just the same as everyone else. We can't be switched on and off or put on standby mode until the next big match. We live with the same ups, downs, needs and emotions. It's just that we operate in a strange world where the only guarantee is uncertainty and the most important currency is goals.

Not long after seeing what remained of the Ferrari, I was back on the football pitch. My legs were like jelly, my lungs all over the place. But I didn't care. To be out there playing was something else. I felt alive. I felt excited. I felt human. Because that's what footballers are. Humans, not robots. We don't live our lives on factory settings. We're an ever-changing swirl of emotions. We feel joy, we feel pain. We feel loved, we feel hurt. We dance like maniacs. We curl up and cry alone in dark rooms.

We are you and you are us – all that separates us is the few inches of whitewash we step across on a matchday. I thank my crash for giving me the opportunity, finally, to show you how, and why.

ONE
LOST IN VICTORY

'Mikey! Come on! Let's go!'

'Uh? What?' I open my eyes. A few of the boys are shaking me, trying to wake me up.

'Come on! We're going out!'

It's more than three hours since the Europa Conference League Final finished, but as the team coach heads towards the middle of Prague at 2 a.m. the boys are still full of it. They should be. They've just done something amazing, something a few of them might never experience again. Me? I can't keep my eyes open.

'I'm not coming,' I tell them. 'I'm going back to the hotel.' I lean into my seat and go back to sleep. At least I try. The boys aren't having it. They're proper goading me. The two Czech lads, Vladimír Coufal and Tomáš Souček, have organised a party. Makes sense, this is their backyard after all.

'Mikey,' they're saying, 'you always organise the parties for us. This is the first time we've actually managed to organise a party for you! You have to come!'

Their confusion at my reluctance is understandable. Everyone knows I like a drink and a party. But, right now, me going out is one of the worst things I can imagine. My body, my mind, my soul is completely against it. The party animal in me is long gone. While the celebrations were going on at the ground, it slunk off quietly into the distance.

The full-time whistle at the Fortuna Arena had sparked absolute mayhem, an explosion of emotion that could have lifted you off your feet. Understandably, after 43 years without a trophy, the West Ham fans were going mad. On the pitch the boys were screaming, hugging one another. In the middle of all that chaos I'd searched out my brother, Duke. When I saw him, I gave him a massive hug. We were both so happy, all we could do was cry. All the emotion, everything we'd been through together, all the hard work, the ups and downs, the endless setbacks, just came pouring out. At that point I was me. I was in the moment like everyone else. I was experiencing what so many footballers never get to experience. I'd won a big European cup competition. I'd fought all my footballing life for this feeling. I was so happy.

And then the bubble burst.

There was another, unseen, element to my life, far removed from the glamour of the Premier League, the great nights of European football. Behind the scenes, my marriage was falling apart. The sheer adrenalin of the match had allowed me a mental escape from all the divorce talk. But when, before the presentation ceremony, two of my kids came down on to the pitch, me and my former partner ended up having an argument, and that was it. From that point on my whole energy was off. Any ability to live in the moment had gone. I just couldn't experience the win. I felt dazed. Lost. It was as if all my problems away from football had smashed straight back into my mind. You've had your fun, Michail. The game's over now. This is your reality, right here.

In the changing room I'd grabbed a couple of drinks. OK, let's see if they liven me up. They didn't. They had no effect whatsoever. All I felt was flat. As a footballer, a night like this is something you dream of. Ultimately, you play football to be there on the greatest occasions. More than that, to actually win something. I kept questioning myself. What the hell is going on? Why can't I enjoy it? This is the biggest game of my life, what my entire playing career has been building up to. And yet, right here, right now, I feel nothing. Can't enter into it. Can't enjoy it. I should feel better than this. I should be happy. I shouldn't feel so drained, so shattered. The energy from winning should have given me enough of a buzz to last hours, like the other players. Instead, I'm gone. I'm not in the same headspace as them. I'm not even on the same planet. What the hell is wrong with me?

And so there I am, on the bus, Tomáš and Vladi still pleading with me. I understand how much they want me with them. How weird it must seem to them that, of all their teammates, it's me who's bailing on the party they've put their efforts into organising. But they're talking to a brick wall. I can't pick myself up off that coach. Can't find anything even remotely resembling motivation. I'm a dead weight. I just need to shut down. And that's what happens. Eventually, Vladi, Tomáš and the rest of the boys give up. They disappear into the night, the coach starts moving and I go back to sleep.

Back at the hotel, I wander down the corridors and find my room. We've just won the Europa Conference League Final and there I am, putting myself to bed. It's a tough place to be when you're behind a hotel room door, in your own head, with your own thoughts, on a night that's supposed to be the biggest ever of your footballing life. Thankfully, exhaustion takes over, sleep comes quickly. It's exactly what I need. I'm suffering from complete emotional wipeout. I can't take any more.

When I open my eyes, the room is light. I decide to go down for breakfast. All the boys are talking about last night. Some of them have only just come in.

They're telling me what a great time they've all had. Normally, I can get a bit of FOMO. Any other time I'd be like, I can't believe I missed that! And for a few seconds I do start thinking that I should have tried to enjoy the moment more, because chances are it won't be something I'll ever experience again. But underneath, I still feel like I've done the right thing. Who knows? Maybe if I had gone out and got drunk, I'd have done something silly. And anyway, I couldn't have made myself go out even if I'd wanted to. I was in complete shutdown mode.

None of the players ask me what was wrong. In fact, only one person has noticed what's really gone on – Josh Ewens, one of the sports scientists. I've known him for 10 years, so he understands me and some of the stuff I'm going through. 'I could just see in you that you weren't right,' he tells me. 'Everyone else was buzzing, drinking and enjoying themselves but you just seemed drained. Not drained by the game – I've seen you tired from a game. Drained by life.'

When he says this to me, I get emotional. I want to cry. It's so powerful, because in those few words he identifies exactly what I'm feeling.

Drained by life. Even football can't save you when that's what you're like.

I'm sure when tales are told of that great victory in Prague, every West Ham fan will think I was there with them partying the night away. But the reality was the complete opposite. I should have been there. I should have been flying. I should have been through the roof … But that's not how your mind reacts when you're under stress. You can block trauma, you can push it to the side as much as you want, but when your brain says it's time to deal with stuff, then it's time. Truth is, I'd emotionally shut down. Become numb. Blocked my feelings out rather than deal with them at the time. I get it. It's a defence mechanism. Remove yourself from the situation. Shut yourself away from it. In the moment it works. But life doesn't exist in a moment. Problems don't just go away. What happens when the situation returns? Numbness isn't a long-term option.

While I actually felt OK during the final itself – the adrenalin of playing in such a massive game kicked in and blanked out everything else that was going on – the period around the match was the first time in my career when I found myself unable to focus on my football and put my everyday life to one side. I just couldn't black out what was going on in the real world. I was pushing my emotions down, but as much as I tried telling myself my issues weren't affecting my game, I knew absolutely that they were. Everything on the field seemed so much more forced. I'd lost the ability to enjoy myself, to express myself freely.

The situation had reached its lowest point the previous December. I found myself stood on the pitch – my happy place – thinking very clearly, *I'm not enjoying this anymore.*

It was a massive shock. Football, the thing that had always filled me up, was now leaving me empty. My passion, something which I'd always seen as non-negotiable, had drained away. I couldn't believe the words bouncing around my head – *I'm not enjoying football*. How could that ever be the case? I'm the most positive person I know. To find myself stood in a stadium, in the middle of a game, in the biggest, most successful, league in the world, and be wishing I wasn't there, was like being smashed in the face with a wrecking ball. I tried to dismiss it, put it out of my mind, but when you're struck by something with so much power it's impossible. I couldn't wait to get out of there.

Afterwards, I was overtaken by another alien feeling – a desire to go on social media. Something I generally avoid like the plague. I know only too well the kind of negative crap that finds oxygen on there. But this time I couldn't stop myself. It was like a compulsion. I absolutely needed to see what was being said about me. I picked up my phone and there it all was, the usual flood of nonsense about how I was yesterday's man, that the best thing West Ham could do was get rid of me. Usually, I can dismiss this kind of stuff as the irrelevant background noise it obviously is. But then I saw another comment. 'He needs to finish right now.' It really landed with me, to the point where I found myself thinking, *You know what? Maybe I should.* I just felt so run-down. My energy, my love of life, of football, had gone. The unthinkable had happened. It was a danger moment. The game has always been my therapy, a way for me to escape any problems going on in my life. As soon as I cross that line, I forget everything that's happening on the other side. But now the escape route was blocked. I couldn't find the freedom I so desperately needed. That left me in a vicious circle. Normally, when my life outside the game is off, my football is doing well. Now my football was going downhill too. I had nothing to give me the pure happiness I craved.

Honestly, I didn't know what was happening to me. I felt like my mind wouldn't switch off. It was on overdrive, my thoughts constantly racing. It was overwhelming. I needed to step away from football, but how could I? I couldn't just say, 'I'm having a few weeks off here, I'll be back to resume my position up top when I feel ready.' As a footballer, you can't just take a few days off and go on holiday. The only time you get off is in the summer, or for an international break – so long as you're not playing. Football's relentless. It goes on and on whatever's happening in your private life. Ask for time off and you're seen as weak, as someone who can't deal with the pressure. Anyway, I needed to be in that team. I was in my thirties. In football that's not a time when you can be taking your foot off the gas. If you want that next contract you need to be performing, not disappearing down a black hole in your own head. I wanted to be in the Premier League, not plunging through its trapdoor like I'd seen so many players do before. I was as frightened as I was confused.

Thankfully, I had a few close people around me who could see I wasn't right and nursed me through that period, talking positively to me, making me see that little glimpse of sunlight through the clouds. Because of them I managed to keep going, putting the boots on and getting out there and playing. But I wasn't right, and it showed in my football. Weeks went by without me sticking the ball in the net. Inevitably I was in and out of the side, each team sheet with my name missing acting as another sharp reminder of my pain.

Help is available in football. Sports psychologists are made available to players at most clubs. A lot of footballers tend to avoid them. Not only do they worry they're going to look feeble if they seek help with their mental health, but there's the issue of trust, the sneaking suspicion that what they say might find its way back to those in charge. Thankfully, at West Ham there was a physio I could trust. I told it to him straight. 'I feel like I'm getting depressed.' Astute bloke that he is, he already knew something was wrong, that I just wasn't myself. We sat and talked and, for the first time, I shared my feelings with someone within my own environment. I needed that conversation, because football isn't a good place for levelling your emotions. It's a game of constant ups and downs. One minute you're flying, the next you're feeling lower than you've ever been. It's hard to deal with at the best of times, let alone when you're struggling to breathe beneath the sheer weight of stress.

To have an outlet like the physio was massive, a valve I could reach for to release at least some of the pressure, but otherwise I kept what I was going through hidden. So, if anyone asked me how I was, I'd just say 'Fine', and that was that. Which suited me, I didn't want people knowing what was going on. Keeping my emotions locked away was my factory setting. What I hadn't realised is that factory settings are there to be adapted, added to, made better. Like most people, I'm constantly updating every bit of tech I have in my life, but when it came to my internal dialogue – my own thoughts on who I was and how I could adapt – I'd never even considered doing such a thing. In football I'd done it constantly. But in life I was operating on an out of date set of processes and procedures. I needed to change.

And the only way to do that was to go back to the beginning.

TWO

WHO AM I?

I've got a trial at QPR. 'Do well in this game,' I'm told, 'and we'll sign you.'

I do well. Two assists. Surely that's going to be enough. But the coach feels differently. 'You didn't put in enough crosses,' he tells me.

I'm pissed off. I've created two goals and that's all he can say to me? 'I could have put in 30 crosses and none of them come to anything,' I tell him. 'Two assists means two goals.'

He's not having it. 'You didn't put in enough crosses so that's that. We're not signing you.'

I walk away. I'm angry, dejected, all of that stuff. But I won't give up the fight.

I never watched football on TV when I was growing up. Never supported a team. I didn't want to waste time sat in front of the telly; it just made me jealous that other people were playing and I wasn't. My life was football, football, football. I either had a ball in my arms or at my feet. Football was always my hobby, and then eventually, 10 years on from first properly kicking a ball at the age of eight, I managed to make that hobby a job.

When I went to Reading, my first professional club, Michael Duberry, the former Chelsea defender, would take the mick out of me because I knew so little about the game. I couldn't say who were the big players, what team they played for, nothing. I'd like to say I remedied that immediately, swatting up on everything football-related. But it wouldn't be true. By the time I arrived at West Ham seven years later, I wasn't much different. The fact there were big names in that dressing room such as Mark Noble, Andy Carroll and Manuel Lanzini didn't bother me in the slightest. I didn't really know who they were. That naivety would work in my favour. When I came off the subs' bench at Manchester City for my West Ham debut, I didn't know who their players were either. Starting out in football, I'd recommend this player blindness to anyone. Rather than worry about someone else, the only focus you have is on yourself. And that's how it was that whole first season in the Premier League. I wasn't intimidated by any opponent, because they meant nothing to me. Their name, their reputation, was totally irrelevant. It would be a couple of years before I realised that it might be to my benefit to know more about an opposition player, how they like to play, and how they might try to stop me playing.

I know my initial ignorance of the game's biggest names might sound mad, but my football journey isn't like that of most other players. My family have no understanding of football whatsoever. They're just not interested. I'll still get a call from one of my brothers on a Friday night asking, 'Do you fancy going out tonight?' I'm like, 'What!? You do understand I've got a game tomorrow!?' The fact I'm a successful footballer who's played at the top of the game makes no difference at all to the Antonio clan. I've never been treated as anything special. To them I'm not Michail Antonio the football star, I'm Michail Antonio the youngest brother. The first thing anyone says to me when we get together is, 'Go and make a cup of tea!' As far as they're concerned, I'm the baby and that's how it is. Football just isn't part of the equation. Very rarely did my parents ever watch me in a match. My mum went along to one of my games when I was 12, and they both came to see me play for Sheffield Wednesday in an away game at Charlton, but even though they were buzzing when they could hear the Wednesday fans singing my name they never did it again, not even when I made it to the Premier League with West Ham. I don't think they understood the nature, the size, of what I was involved in until I was called up by England. Not that it ever bothered me. It was just something I was used to. People have said to me again and again, 'Michail, you're so grounded.' But my family kept me that way.

As a kid, maybe that family disinterest in the game rubbed off on me a bit. There was a time when I was more interested in chess than football. Struggling in school with maths, I found chess, the ultimate test of tactics, was something I could focus on. By the age of nine, though, I knew I had talent on the playground. I was holding my own with kids who were two years older than me. From that point on, if anyone asked me what I wanted to be, there was only one answer – 'Footballer!'

'OK, and if that doesn't happen?'

I never answered that question. To me there wasn't an 'if'. IT WAS GOING TO HAPPEN! I met up with my old primary school headteacher, Mr Troy, a few years ago and his description of me at that age was simple – 'Football! Football! Football!' First into the playground with a ball, last out of the playground with a ball, as he put it 'sometimes kicking and screaming'. And he was right. I always had a ball in my hand, out there playing with my friends. Mr Troy was very kind about me that day I met him. He didn't mention that I had another hobby as well as playing football. Talking. A lot. I'm sure he must have spent a lot of time rolling his eyes at me.

I remember those days as a small kid well. I'd be in the 'cages', the artificial pitches surrounded by chain fences, or in the park, classic thing, coats as goalposts. It was there I was spotted by the Tooting & Mitcham junior management. I was 11. I started going to training and that was that.

Tooting & Mitcham was the start of me heading off down a very different path to a lot of other players my age. By that time a lot of kids have been sucked into the academy system where professional clubs look to nurture promising young talent through to the first team. There was none of that with me. Other than school teams, before the age of 12 I hadn't played for anyone. Tooting & Mitcham might not have happened either. My mum was unhappy because the games were on a Sunday. Mum was very religious. I mean proper religious. Every Sunday I'd be there, suited and booted, at church. I'd even sing in the choir. Being allowed to play football instead was a real battle. The manager had to knock on the door and get my mum's permission. If he hadn't done that and told her he'd look after me until she got back from church, there's no way I could have played.

The weirdest experience I had as a teenage footballer was going to Russia to take part in a youth tournament. I was training with Chelsea Kicks, part of Chelsea's community programme at the time, down at Providence House, a youth and community centre near Clapham Junction station, when the coaches announced there was a tournament coming up in Moscow. 'Would you be OK to go?' I didn't need asking twice. 'Yeah, why not?'

That first morning in Russia I looked out the hotel window and could see nothing but lovely blue skies. Classic T-shirt weather. And then I stepped outside the door. Absolutely freezing! I'd kind of forgotten we were 1,500 miles east of Clapham. 'Oh my God! I need to go back to my room and get my jacket.'

'No chance,' I was told. 'We're running late. You can't go back.'

Player power isn't a thing when you're 14 and so that was that. We set off walking round the city. It was *so* cold. No way could I deal with it. My mum had given me a little bit of spending money. I was so fed up. *Am I really going to use up all my money on the first day – on a jacket? I'm going to have to!* That was it. I literally had nothing left for the rest of the time we were there.

There was something else I noticed early on. Everyone was staring at us, and I don't think it was because of my new jacket. Other than a couple of white boys, the trip was 15 Black lads. It was as if aliens had landed. Everyone breaking their necks, turning around, looking at us, as if to say, 'What on Earth are you guys doing here?' We were pretty wide-eyed ourselves. Everything we looked at in the shops or markets seemed to double as a weapon. At one point I was looking at a lighter when the stallholder told me, 'Press that button!' I did as he said and a knife shot out the bottom. *What the ...?* It was absolutely crazy.

That first evening, the mayor invited us out to a posh restaurant. We'd only been on the minibus a few minutes when the police pulled us over. Before we knew it, they were climbing aboard. A run-in with the authorities is worrying enough at the best of times, but these were a bunch of unpredictable Russian cops armed with some serious-looking guns. 'You!' they pointed at one of the players. 'Off the bus!' He was absolutely pooing himself, as, truth be told, were the rest of us. *What's going on here?* We needn't have worried. It turned out they'd done it to shit us up more than anything – and they succeeded. I didn't fancy spending my life rotting in a Russian prison. ('Anyone know what happened to Michail?' 'Yeah, don't you remember? He went to play a game in Russia 20 years ago and never came back.') I was definitely not getting up to any mischief over there, which is why when word got round of a strip joint in the hotel I, for one, stayed very firmly put in my room.

Back in the more familiar surroundings of home, I'd watch as other players were selected for various academies. Luck just never seemed to fall my way. The same day Fulham came down to Providence House to have a look at the talent, my mum took me to a christening. Practically everyone who was there that day got signed, which meant when they came back the following week their quota was full. 'If you'd been here last week, we'd have signed you,' they told me. When you've missed out on your dream, it's the last thing you want to hear.

But there was always hope. In fact, more than hope. By the time I was 14, I was getting the attention I craved from scouts linked to professional clubs. I was blown away to be offered a trial by Tottenham. *Bloody hell, the big-time!* Except I never got there. Mum feared it would affect my schoolwork. Her attitude was uncompromising. 'Education comes first!' To say I was gutted would be an understatement. The way I saw it, she had quite literally taken my future in football away from me. I was properly in tears. I mean, who turns down Tottenham? Maybe that was it, my big chance gone. At the same time, I could kind of see where she was coming from. Spurs wasn't exactly on the doorstep for a kid living in south London, and training with them after school would mean me not getting home until practically midnight. Also, she was totally right in thinking I needed a back-up. Not committing to Spurs meant I studied for and got a sports diploma, which would have come in handy had I not made it in football. And it wasn't like she was putting the kybosh on my ambition full-stop. She did believe in me. For a long time, it was her paying for my boots. They were the cheap plastic ones that only lasted a few games before getting all busted up, but it was all she could afford and I was grateful for her support. Mum might not have cared about football, but she wanted me to be happy.

As I progressed, I had trials at a few other London clubs. After the debacle at QPR, I went to Brentford, only to be told a similar story. I played two games and got an assist and a goal. The message this time was, 'You've got potential, but we're not going to sign you.' It made no sense. If a club can see the potential in a player, why wouldn't they invest in them? Take them to the next level? For so long, it felt like every single player was being invited to join one academy or another. Every single player but me.

Now, of course, I realise that constant rejection was the best thing that could have happened to me. Getting knock-backs toughened me up. It gave me a hard edge, a resilience, that can sometimes be lacking in those who come through the academy system, simply because they get it way too easy. Obviously, the battle to get a pro-contract is hard, but everything else is weighted in their favour. It's not that long since academy lads were cleaning the changing room, washing the senior players' boots. They had to do the graft before they got the benefits. Now they're pampered from the age of 13 or 14. The result is by the time they reach the first team they're not as hungry as they should be. They've already got so much, so why would they be? Compare that to me. While they were in that comfort zone, I was pushing myself, learning not to take no for an answer. If I got a rejection at one door, I moved on and knocked on the next one. My attitude was simple. *You don't think I'm good enough? I'll prove you wrong.* That wasn't me being arrogant, it was me knowing I had the ability. No-one likes getting knockbacks, but I was never going to let them stop me. My attitude then was the same as now. If you believe something will happen – truly believe – then there's every chance it will come to pass.

That battle to get to the next stage, for my talent to be recognised, was even played out on my own doorstep. At Tooting & Mitcham, I played for every age group without ever getting in the actual youth team, as the manager preferred to bring in players from outside. In the end I trialled for that youth team, successfully, off my own back. I wore the number 14 shirt, the same as one of the few footballing heroes I did recognise and adore, Thierry Henry. By then I'd started my growth spurt. Up until the age of 15 I was small and skinny, so my game was all about skill and pace. Within a year my body shape completely changed. A few years ago, I caused great hilarity on Gary Lineker's *The Rest is Football* podcast when I blurted out that, in the following 12 months, I grew six inches 'all over'. What I was trying to say was I bulked up and added power to my skillset.

From the youth team I went pretty much straight away to the reserves, before meeting yet more resistance. While the reserve-team boss recommended me to the first-team manager, the step-up was thought too much for me. I was seen as nothing more than a kid and no way would I have the strength or ability to handle it. And so I did the same as I'd done with the youth team. Independently, I took myself to a trial. And guess what? They liked what they saw and offered me a contract. Not that I was going to take it. The last thing I wanted to do was to sign for them and, if they then stuck a high price on me, kill the move to a professional club that I was sure was just round the corner. They weren't too happy with that and so effectively kicked me out – if I wasn't going to sign a contract then I'd have to leave the club. When AFC Wimbledon then showed an interest, I thought I'd made the right decision. Finally, I was on my way. Well, I would have been, were it not for the small matter of seven quid. That was the amount they refused to pay for my registration fee. Seven quid might not seem much, but no way was I paying it. I wasn't exactly flush at that stage and I'd heard that Wimbledon, powering their way through non-league, were paying players a grand a week. More than anything it was the principle of the thing. I was going to their reserves, not their first team. Paying my own money to do something that felt a little bit of a backwards step just felt wrong.

Back at Tooting & Mitcham I signed their contract – £150 a week tax-free. I'll be honest, at this point I did have doubts whether I would make it as a pro. I was looking round at friends who were all working, earning decent money. Thoughts did enter my head. *Do I keep on trying to make this work? How long can I carry on for?* By now my dad was also saying the time had come to stop thinking about football and get a real job. He'd always thought pursuing a football career was pointless. Dad was more of a cricket guy. He loved the West Indies team, although if they were touring

England he wouldn't do what most Jamaicans would and grab the opportunity to watch them down the road at The Oval. He thought paying for tickets for things like that was a waste; he wanted to put his money into the house and into us. To be fair, he was only being realistic. Times were tough. It wasn't like there was loads of cash around, one reason why he was sick of me asking for money off him for better boots or whatever.

In an alternate universe where football didn't happen for me, possibly I'd have been a PE teacher. I applied to two universities, Southampton and Kingston, to do sports science. More likely I'd have been working for my brother John in his building company. John was himself a very good footballer, but he left it behind because he wanted to go into business. He was adamant, however, that my own footballing journey shouldn't end in the nine-to-five. Two years older, John's like a best friend to me, always my first port of call whenever I've hit one of life's crossroads. His message was clear: 'You're way too good to be thinking about giving up.' It was classic John, the person who, more than anyone, is responsible for where I am today. In fact, he might be responsible for me being alive.

This might seem a strange thing to say, but when I was growing up, people being stabbed was an everyday thing. You'd hear it all the time. 'So-and-so got stabbed the other day.' It was totally run of the mill, so much so that you'd hear about a knifing and your reaction wouldn't be one of surprise, it would be, 'Oh, right, where did that happen?' That was the extent of the conversation. Not even, 'Is the person OK?'

That is, until it happened to Eugene. He was a friend who I used to play football with. And then, aged just 16, he was murdered. Eugene belonged to a gang called the SUK (Stick 'Em Up Kids) and was set upon by seven or eight youths from a rival gang called TZ (Terror Zone). A teenager was later jailed for life for his murder. Eugene was my first experience of death. And it was scary. At that moment, the whole idea of dying suddenly became very real, very clear. Yes, I'd hear about people getting stabbed, but usually it was a wound in the leg, or the arm. Eugene got stabbed in the chest, back and head. Many times. There was no way he was going to survive. His whole future stolen from him in a single horrific moment.

There was something else about Eugene's death. In different circumstances it could have been me.

I didn't grow up with lots of money or in a particularly great part of south London. Gangs were a fact of life where I lived and the streets often felt dangerous. Every day meant constant uncertainty. Take a wrong turn and there was every chance you could be attacked or robbed. To defend yourself you might end up having to fight. And it wasn't just on the streets where gangs existed. School was a mirror of what was happening outside. The SUK, from Clapham Junction, and TZ, from Tooting & Mitcham, were there as well.

I was definitely a fighter. I hadn't learned how to handle my feelings at that stage. There's been times in my life when I've been pretty much constantly upbeat while hurting badly on the inside. I've had to learn that when you're down it's OK to let your emotion come out, because if it doesn't come out one way it'll come out in another. As I've got older, I've realised that's what happened when I was younger. Even though I had people I could speak to around me, I never really opened up about my emotions, because I never felt comfortable doing it. I was a boy. You didn't show emotion if you were a boy. 'Big boys don't cry' – you heard that all the time. And what does it really mean? 'Hold your emotions in. Don't ever show you're hurt.' Problem is, while you're keeping that stuff inside, all you're doing is digging a deeper and deeper hole for yourself.

I had a lot of resentment, a lot of pent-up emotion, because I never got to express myself properly, and that frustration came out in another way. I had a short temper. I could lose it quickly, and I would fight with people all the time. If someone said something I didn't like, I'd tell them to stop. And they weren't getting two warnings. Carry on, and they were getting hit. At the same time, my emotional side was desperate to show itself. Whenever I got angry, I cried. In the house, it wasn't unknown for me to run out of a room in tears. Those same tears would come before a scrap. Which would make me want to fight even more. That person had made me look small, and so I needed to show them I was the exact opposite.

I get that fighting sounds bad, but if I hadn't stood up for myself, especially as a smaller kid, I'd have been pushed around. Let people do that and soon they're taking it to another level. I saw kids who couldn't fend for themselves getting bullied. I needed people to realise I wasn't someone to be messed with. And that's what happened. No-one ever really troubled me. I'll be honest, being able to handle myself, and being surrounded by gangs, meant there were times I was tempted to go down the same path. People in those gangs were making money. They dressed good. They had girls around them – the whole 'bad boy' thing. So, yes, it did appeal to me.

What kept me away from all that was my brother John. He was never interested in any of that gang stuff. When I spoke to him, his attitude was simple. 'Why limit yourself in life? Why prevent yourself from being able to go from one place to another when you could have friends from all over? There's a gang in Brixton, a gang in Croydon, a gang everywhere. Join one, and that's it, you're trapped.' What he said made total sense, especially since I had friends in both the SUK and TZ. Living in Earlsfield, 10 minutes from Tooting and 15 from Clapham Junction, I was in the worst position to join either, sat bang in the middle. At one stage the two gangs united. It was a brief pause in hostilities. A month later they were back fighting. The message was clear. If you were in one gang's territory, you couldn't go into the other.

From the moment John pointed out how being in a gang would control my every move, my mind was clear. I wasn't going to join any crew. It was the best thing I could have done, because it meant there was no territorial reason for me not to play for Tooting & Mitcham, my eventual route into professional football. I could also head over to Providence House youth club at Clapham Junction, an oasis of calm in a troubled area. There were estates nearby where stabbings, even shootings, weren't uncommon. But because of the respect the kids had for the people in charge of the youth club, there was never any trouble. Kids valued that space. One time somebody sprayed graffiti on the door and the kids themselves made sure the person who'd done it cleaned it up. That togetherness was built by Robert Musgrave who ran the place. I call him 'the daddy of Clapham Junction' because it feels like he raised everyone round there. Robert believed in kids and so allowed them to believe in themselves. He showed them what was possible – the talent, for all sorts of things, they had within. If I didn't have any money, he might also give me a couple of free things from the tuckshop. I played at Providence House for five years. It still does amazing work helping young people find all sorts of different paths through life; showing that friendship and togetherness is what builds a safe community.

Essentially, away from gangs I felt like I could roam free. Doing whatever I wanted, with no restrictions, meant I was even going as far afield as Norbury, out towards Croydon, to play there. Alongside that freedom, I was seeing how much the world around me was changing. Fist fights were becoming a thing of the past; knives were now so present in society. I came to a realisation. *Is it really worth me risking my life over something that someone's said to me? I'd rather live and not fight than ever want to fight and die.* I couldn't ever see myself being able to stab somebody. I could never have that in me. Once fighting meant bringing a knife, I was not about that life. It wasn't about the difference between right and wrong being instilled in me by my parents, it came from within. I never wanted to hurt anybody; I could never imagine plunging a blade into someone. The thought of sticking a knife in raw chicken felt awful to me, let alone another person. Even now I can't watch if somebody is sticking a needle in me. I can't deal with that type of stuff. To this day, if I find myself in a bad or dangerous situation, I'll always try my hardest to talk to the other person. I'd only ever get physical if there was no other way out and I was forced to protect myself. In a time when there's people with knives, people with guns, it's just not worth it.

My brush with gangs came 20 years ago. Sadly, little has changed. Knife crime is still a massive part of life – and death – in south London. Growing up round there, and in plenty of other parts of the UK, it's easy to get sucked into gang culture. Gangs promise money and popularity. I hope I can show kids that there's another way. Do your own thing and good things can happen. In my case, football gave me a focus, something to aim for. Sport has a massive role to play in keeping kids off the streets. It stops people getting into gangs and into fights. I hope, as someone who grew up on those same streets, kids can see it is possible to turn your back on the bad stuff and go on to achieve something. I've been back to my old secondary school, Southfields Academy, and Providence House, to help spread that message. Footballers aren't robots and neither are kids. With guidance, they can make the right choices.

I had that guidance from John. He never ever stopped making me believe, and he backed up his words by buying me my first pair of proper football boots, Nike Total 90s, like Wayne Rooney's, costing about £150. 'Right, you've got the boots,' he told me, 'now go out and smash it!' And that's what I did. Nine appearances for Tooting & Mitcham later, I'd scored 10 goals. I was on fire, to the extent that after a game against Millwall reserves, the League One club told me they wanted me at their training ground the next day. I did three days with Millwall and that was enough for them to offer me a contract. At the same time, Tooting & Mitcham also recommended me to Steve Coppell, the manager at Reading. I played a trial game for the Royals and they too offered me terms. All that time fighting for recognition and now, in the space of a few days, I'd got two well-established professional clubs wanting me. Reading, at that point, were in the Championship. Signing for them was a no-brainer. In fact, it was so exciting that I couldn't sleep the night before. When the next day came, and I had the pen in my hand to put my signature to a two-year deal, I did so in those same Total 90s my brother had bought me. Finally, I could say to my parents, 'Mum, Dad, I'm officially getting paid to play football.'

Looking back now, I'm so happy with the route I took into professional football. It allowed me that little bit more time living as a normal kid, rather than what I saw happen to so many other young players. One minute they were having fun, the next they'd disappeared into an academy and that was that. We're talking about kids as young as 11. Lives put on hold. Training, training, training. No guarantee of anything at the end of it. And all the time missing out on what being a kid should be about – having fun with your mates. I, on the other hand, was 18 by the time I got signed. Other than Ian Wright, another massive hero of mine, I was hard pushed to think of another player who'd come into the pro game that late. Today, clubs have realised the potential of non-league and so it's more common to see players getting in through that route. But back then it hardly ever happened. The fact I was never an academy kid will always be in my favour. My late entry into a solid football routine meant not only had I enjoyed a childhood but, like generations of wannabe footballers before me, I'd had to fight for everything. Mine was a far bumpier road to the top than practically every other pro I encountered, which I believe made me more effective and mentally stronger than a lot of players who'd been wrapped up in cotton wool. I'm not the only one to bear that out. Look at Jamie Vardy and Charlie Austin, tough, tough players with passion and determination by the bucketload. No wonder clubs are looking more and more at players who learned their trade the hard way. They're cheaper, hugely ambitious and are incredibly robust.

Whenever a kid says to me they haven't played academy football, my message is always the same. 'Don't give up! The thick skin you develop outside the academy system is your superpower.' I took the never-say-die attitude I learned as a kid all the way with me into professional football. If a new manager came in and left me on the sidelines, straight away I'd set about proving them wrong. *I WILL change their mind. They WILL have to put me in the team.* And it worked. I've never had a manager who, sooner or later, didn't play me. More than that, they were playing me week in, week out.

It didn't stop at managers. Players have doubted me too. During my time at West Ham, for instance, I had fellow players say to me, 'You're lucky to be here.' Ginge, otherwise known as our defender James Collins, would tell me that all the time – seriously, not taking the piss. He honestly didn't believe I was good enough to be at the club. My comeback to him or anyone else who said that, was always the same. 'I believe I'm one of the best players here.' It never affected me, because I always listened to my own voice more than theirs. I could tell myself I wasn't lucky, I deserved it. And the facts bore that out. I've never been at a club where I wasn't an important cog in the wheel. I've been one of the best wherever I've been. Whoever it might be, players or managers, I've always proven to them I can get the job done.

Although 'getting the job done' didn't happen straight away.

THREE
THE GAME

You feel it before you see it. When it comes to that
nagging feeling you're being edged towards the door,
you don't need someone to tell you or to read it on
the back page of the newspaper. The vibe is all
around. There's talk of 'refreshing the style of play'
or 'adding something new to the squad'. But, of
course, squads can't keep growing and growing.
Makes sense that if you're going to add something,
then something else has to be taken away.

People think the most difficult hurdle in professional football is getting noticed by a professional team and signing that longed-for contract. It isn't. The most difficult thing is staying there when you get there. There's a constant stream of young players coming through, wanting to take your spot. A phenomenal number of players get released every year. The vast majority of footballers will get nowhere near the Premier

League. The bigger concern is that they'll end up out of football and have to start over in the world of work. Think about it, there's only 11 numbers. Yes, there's the squad, but if you're not making that starting 11 you're eventually going to get thrown away. You need to be playing if the people that matter are going to respect you and want to keep you. Unless that's happening, you're never going to be safe.

With so much riding on it (this was my dream, and I didn't want to balls it up), despite the difference in size between the clubs, I found it much harder walking through the door at Reading than I did seven years later at West Ham. I was more nervous of the opportunity than anything else. By signing for the Royals, in one fell swoop I'd leapfrogged five divisions. Reading had only been relegated from the Premier League the season before. They were a force to be reckoned with and easily reached the Championship play-offs that year. I, meanwhile, had arrived at the Madejski Stadium straight from the Isthmian League Premier Division. The difference in quality hit me like a thunderbolt between the eyes. When I wandered out on to the training pitch that first day, I thought I'd be training with the reserves or Under-21s. 'No, no,' I was told, 'you're over there with the first team.' *What?* I was playing it cool, but inside I felt so nervous. There were some big names at Reading, players like Kevin Doyle, Stephen Hunt, Michael Duberry and Leroy Lita. And there was me – an unknown from non-league. Never played in an academy or anything.

To say it was straight in at the deep end would be putting it mildly. At Tooting & Mitcham, there were days when I wouldn't even go into training. More often than not it would just be a few passing drills, and anyway when matchday came round I knew I'd be playing. At Reading, however, training was full-on and challenging. There was a drill called 'Keep Ball', exactly as it sounds: one team keeps the ball from the other, passing it on quickly in a tiny box just a few metres square. It was a concept totally alien to me. I was a winger, all about getting from one end of the pitch to the other, putting a cross in, making an assist, or scoring a goal. This box I now found myself in might as well have been a prison – a very full prison. Five players on each side hellbent on keeping the ball. Well, five players on one side and four on the other, in this case. As a winger, my instinct was to get the ball, look up and then pass. I'd be about half a second into that process and the ball would be taken off my foot. The other boys were so frustrated with me. It was like being back in the playground. 'We don't want him on our team!' So the next time I got the ball, I dug my heels into the ground to protect it, got my head up and tried to look for the pass. I'd kept the ball but now I was fighting off two players on my back. Assistant manager Nigel Gibbs came over. 'You need to know where you're going to pass the ball before you receive it. You can't just get it and then put your head up. That's too late. By then you're going to be surrounded.' These were exactly the things I needed to learn. Same as how, training in a more familiar style as a winger, I'd take people on only for my technique to let me down, shanking the ball out of play or messing up in some other way. I expect that, in the same situation, other players might have let their heads go down. But if there was one thing I always believed in, it was myself and my ability to score goals. Thankfully, in the regular five-a-side sessions I was able to better show what I was all about; that the club had signed me for a reason.

A fast-track to improvement is sending a player out on loan, and that's exactly what happened to me. I'm not sure it's something all players enjoy, but early in my career I much preferred going on loan than staying where I was and playing for the reserves. I wanted to be challenged, to learn my trade by playing professional football under pressure. Playing for the reserves or Under-21s, no-one really gets on your back. Making mistakes isn't that big a deal, whereas when you're playing in a first team, errors mean something. The fans are giving you stick, the manager can lose his job, your team-mates are losing bonus money. You're also building your profile. The more you play, the more people see your stats. You're visible. There's a chance to get noticed. No two ways about it, going on loan accelerates development and professional reputation.

Cheltenham Town manager Martin Allen picked me up after spotting my potential in a reserve game at Charlton. In so doing, he gave me my very first professional game opportunity at, of all places, Elland Road, in front of 20,000 highly excitable Leeds United fans desperate for this massive club to drag itself back out of League One after being relegated from the Championship the season before. In a matter of a few months, I'd gone from playing in front of 150 people in non-league to this, one of the most iconic stadiums in English football.

I will never forget that day. I was so nervous. Like, *so* nervous. I still get that anxiousness about me before a big game, but when I'm in the dressing room I manage it by keeping myself to myself, listening to music, slow music, like old-school R&B, zoning myself in – the calm before the storm of the game. At Elland Road, however, it was a trick I was yet to learn. As we walked out on to the pitch, the roar I heard from the Leeds fans was like *Wow!* Now I felt properly nervous. My heart was beating so loud, so fast, I could feel the judders in my chest. But I was so glad I was there. Stepping on to the turf, I said to myself, *I've made it! I really have made it!* Quickly I caught myself. *Actually, I haven't yet. I need to do the job first, right?*

The whistle went and I started unbelievably. Playing right wing, I took my man on a couple times, got a couple of crosses into the box, before beating two men and cutting inside. On the edge of the box, I was on for a shot at goal. At the exact moment I pulled the trigger, a Leeds defender got his foot to the other side of the ball. The force going through my ankle tore three ligaments. Not that I knew it at the time. *OK, what was that? Didn't feel great but let me see how I get on.* I hobbled around for a bit, but the ankle was so sore that eventually I went across to the bench and told the gaffer I was struggling. 'Strap it up!' he shouted. Slowly I started taking my boot off at the side of the pitch and then out of nowhere Martin, clearly frustrated at the time I was taking, appeared and ripped it off my foot. 'Aaaaghhhh!' The pain was so excruciating that I was actually screaming. The physio strapped me up over my sock – no way was that coming off too – before the boot went back on a little less violently than it had come off and I limped back on to the field. I was desperate to stay on but managed just another quarter of an hour before I had to admit defeat. When I inspected my ankle back in the dressing room, it had ballooned to double its normal size. My foot felt like it was hanging off. Barely had I made my debut than I was looking at three months out. The spell at Cheltenham never really got going after that – subbed on, subbed off, not much starting time – but I had another chance to show what I could do when Southampton took me on loan the following season.

Like Leeds, Southampton were another big club plunged into the unfamiliar territory of League One, although they still had some great players, like Rickie Lambert and Adam Lallana. When Reading coach Wally Downes partnered up with Saints boss Alan Pardew, he gave me a call and said they wanted me at St Mary's. It was the move which made my career. I played 39 games that season, a solid block which allowed me to showcase exactly what I could do, scoring seven goals from the wing. For the first time, I felt like I was really contributing. I was part of a team going great guns, starting on minus 10 points after going into administration and finishing in seventh place, just below the play-offs. I also had the unbelievable experience of scoring a goal at Wembley, the fourth in a 4–1 win over Carlisle United in the final of the 2010 Johnstone's Paint Trophy. It was the best 20th birthday present I could have ever wished for. Southampton were looking to sign me, but Reading, impressed with my development, wanted to hang on to a promising player. I started appearing more regularly for them, and after another short loan period at Colchester United, I went out on loan to

Sheffield Wednesday, also in League One, who signed me on a permanent deal.

You might think at that point, three years into my pro career, I would have felt secure. I was, after all, at a big club, enjoying a promotion to the Championship in my first season. But being a footballer means constant instability. You have so little power over your destiny that you might feel totally settled at a club one day and then the next have the rug pulled right from under your feet. The end days at Sheffield Wednesday are a great example. I was there for two-and-a-half years, one of the mainstays, playing week in, week out. I was loving it. I was relaxed. No way did I want to go. And then one day at training the manager, Stuart Gray, came across.

'I'm selling you.'

'What? What are you talking about? How does that work? I'm one of the main players and you're selling me? I don't want to leave!'

He started explaining. 'I think you're better than this club. You're stagnating. Moving on will be good for you.' I wasn't really buying that, which was when he added, 'And I need the money to bring more players in.' OK, now we'd reached the crux of the matter.

It turned out that Nottingham Forest were interested. I went home to tell my wife, Debbie. Unsurprisingly, it came as a shock. 'What do you mean? Do you have to go?'

'Technically, no. But the fact the manager wants to sell me means it's going to be pretty hard to stay.'

While I wasn't expecting to leave, at least Forest were a decent club, desperate, like Wednesday, to get back to the

Premier League. But it was still an upheaval. I was still nervous. At the end of the day, I was comfortable at Hillsborough. Too comfortable according to Gray. 'You need to move on. You need to challenge yourself.'

And so I accepted the move, signing a three-year contract. The result was one of the best years I've ever had. I don't know what they put in the water in Nottingham but I racked up 16 goals for Forest and I'd say nine of them were unbelievable. If you get a chance, take a look at the one I scored against Bolton, beating five men before smashing the ball past the keeper. There were times I was quite literally scoring for fun. My stats were right up there with the best players in the league. Even now I can't understand how I didn't make the EFL Championship Team of the Year.

After such a great season, naturally I was hoping to make the jump to the Premier League. West Brom, then a top-flight side, came in for me, but Forest, under a transfer embargo at the time for failing to meet Financial Fair Play (FFP) regulations, said no. In my mid-twenties, making my dream come true felt like now or never. By then I'd been grafting in the Championship for three years. I'd done everything there was to do in the division. I wanted my opportunity to show what I could do in the Premier League, and I knew it wasn't going to happen with Forest, as they didn't have anywhere near the quality of squad for promotion. 'You need to let me go,' I was telling them, 'I've been waiting for this my entire life.' The result, inevitably, was a bust-up, to the extent I refused to play in the home game against Charlton early the following season. Beforehand, I'd driven to the City Ground and spoken

to the chairman Fawaz Al-Hasawi. I told him I'd play but I
needed to know that the club would let me get a move. By
this point, West Ham had contacted my agent, but we'd told
them not to bid until we sorted out the situation with Forest.
Again, however, I got a refusal. I felt trapped. I was one of the
worst-paid players at the club and now they were going to
make me stay.

'You're under contract and that's the end of it.'

'OK,' I said, 'no problem.'

I got straight back in my car and drove out through the
crowds of fans arriving for the game. Two days later, I went
into the training ground. Dougie Freedman, the manager, had
a word with me. 'Look Michail,' he said, 'I'm here to help
you,' all this stuff about how he understood where I was
coming from and would help me get the move I wanted.
Except, it seemed to me that he was the reason I was going
nowhere. He wanted me to stay because the FFP embargo
meant he was going to struggle to bring in a replacement. It
was at this point that Fawaz arrived. Here we were, all three
of us in the same place. I spotted an opportunity. 'Should we
have a chat?' Dougie claimed to be busy, but I was insistent.
'I'll wait all day if I have to.' Dougie saw saying no was pointless. 'OK,' I asked, 'are you guys going to tell me what's going
on?'

Dougie said he felt I was putting undue pressure on the
owner of the club. I wasn't having that. 'I'm not putting pressure on anybody. I'm just saying I need to move on. It's a
great opportunity for me and my family.' Again, the chairman
started going on about what a great job I was doing at Forest

and how I should fulfil my contract. I pointed out that I was one of the worst-paid players in the place. 'You're telling me I'm the best player at the club, but you want me to stay the worst-paid?'

'There's nothing we can do,' insisted Fawaz. 'Even if we do sell you, we can't spend the money.'

I looked at Dougie. 'But you said you'd help me go.'

With Fawaz there he reverse-ferreted and claimed not to have done so.

'OK,' I said, apologising to the chairman, 'now I know what this is. It's not you, it's him. You're trying to help him out by keeping me. And he's trying to keep me onside by telling me he's going to help me leave.'

I walked out, boiling with anger. On my way to my car, I took my phone out of my pocket. 'If you keep me here,' I texted Dougie, 'the problem is not going to be mine. The problem is going to be yours. Because you can't tell me what tactics you want me to do. I'm going to play my best for me, do all the right things for me, and that's it. In the meantime, don't speak to me, not in the changing room, not at the training ground, not anywhere.'

I got sold two days later.

Of course, fans don't see any of these behind-the-scenes shenanigans. They just read that someone's refused to play and that's that. The insinuation is always that the player is being unreasonable or being greedy. In fact, in a world where we have so little control, we're just trying to do what's best for us. It's our lives. What are we supposed to do? Just go along with this shit? People playing us off against one another. It happens a lot more in football than people might think. A decade on, I'd face exactly the same situation with Graham Potter, although by the time he came through the door at West Ham I was well used to having to defend my position. Always having my head on the swivel. Never able to rest. Who's coming up behind me? What threat am I going to have to fend off next? That might sound a bit over the top, but I was at West Ham for ten years and every single summer the club was talking about replacing me. It was always a case of I wasn't good enough. Or they felt they needed a new approach. I was forever justifying my place in the team. In a decade with the Hammers, not once did I feel like the striker's spot was mine to keep. Not ever. When you're the sort of player who doesn't look particularly pretty, whose technical skills aren't going to get the pundits drooling on *Match of the Day*, it's inevitable that you're having to prove yourself over and over again. Life is one constant fight for your place.

At West Ham, every new manager who came in was unsure about me. Even the one who was there when I arrived had his doubts, because I was the chairman's signing not his. Constant uncertainty is exhausting. The expectation is that if you're going to play professional football you'll get used to it. But getting used to it doesn't mean you have to accept it. I was never going to let someone knock me down easily. I needed to believe I was one of the best in the team. I couldn't ever let myself think that someone was better than me. Do that and I'd lose a massive part of what makes me the player I am. That attitude never wavered. When I got into my mid-thirties, people would say to me 'at your age you should be happy just to be involved'. Why? Just because I was a certain age didn't mean I didn't have what it takes. My body was still in great condition. Mentally, too, my desire remained the same. While that continued to be the case, I was always going to resent other people getting in the team before me. I was always going to fight for my place. Because being out of the team is awful.

What I particularly resented was players getting in the team ahead of me when they didn't deserve it. I saw it time and again at West Ham. A big signing would come in, not perform, and yet the manager would persist with them to justify the amount of money that had been spent. In the meantime, I was sat on the sidelines. As far as I was concerned the money was irrelevant. If they weren't perform-ing, then I should be back in the team doing my job. I should be given that opportunity. It happened with Sébastien Haller in 2019. Manuel Pellegrini brought in the Ivory Coast striker for a club record £45 million and I only got back in when he got injured. No sooner had I regained the frontman position than Pellegrini was sacked. Thankfully, his replacement, David Moyes, saw me as a frontman as well and I finished the season as West Ham's leading scorer with 10 goals despite making just 20 starts in a struggling team. Haller, meanwhile, was moved on 18 months later for half his purchase price after he failed to make the big impact the club was hoping for.

The Italian Gianluca Scamacca was the same. Signed for £30.5 million in 2022, he was gone a year later. To be fair to him and Haller, West Ham didn't play to their strengths. Both needed someone else up front to play off, but we never did that. By the time my own stay in east London was brought to a close, the Germany international Niclas Füllkrug was also struggling to justify his £27 million price tag. West Ham brought in so many different strikers, but no matter how hard they tried they just weren't able to replace me. In the end, the manager would realise what had been clear to me all the time – they needed someone who could, one way or another, stick the ball in the net, and that was me.

That's not to say I never expected there to be competition for my place. Of course I did. This was the Premier League, the best in the world. If you're not doing your job, you're going to get booted. But I never shirked the pressure of being among the elite. Neither did I need it. Any pressure from the outside can never be bigger than the pressure I put on myself. I'm always pushing to achieve. It's when I don't feel that pressure, when I'm settled, comfortable, that I'll play my worst football. That's why I never sit still. I'm constantly trying to improve. I always believe in myself, a characteristic I again trace directly back to my earliest days when I was that kid desperate to get that first contract. No-one giving me a leg-up, making so much of it happen myself. It was an attitude that meant I was never going to compromise. I was never going to sit back and be made to feel unworthy. Never going to accept being made the scapegoat.

When it came to my career, I would always, always, fight.

FOUR

GOOD BOSS, BAD BOSS

I like Dave. I do. I really like him. But right now, in this dressing room at half-time, I'm struggling to remember why.

'You're not f***ing running enough, Michail!' His face is right up against mine. I can see every line, etched in pure anger. He moves an inch nearer. 'For f***'s sake, f***ing run!'

Am I meant to just take this? Again? And again? And again?

'You can't keep shouting at me, every f***ing time,' I tell him. 'There's more than me in this team.'

But he does. He keeps on shouting at me. Every f***ing time.

There are plenty of people who can make a massive difference to a footballer's life. But none can ever wield more influence, positive or negative, than the manager.

There's one boss I played under a fair bit more than anyone else – David Moyes. I had a lot of time for Dave, but if you'd stepped into the West Ham dressing room at half-time on an average matchday you'd have thought we absolutely hated each other. It felt like every single game he'd come in shouting and swearing, and it was pretty much always in my direction. The background might change – one week Tottenham's gleaming white tiles, the next the rather less glamorous changing facilities at Bournemouth – but the message was always the same. 'You're not f***ing running enough, Michail!' Eventually, I started thinking, *This is personal! I can't not be running every f***ing game! How far does this maniac think I can travel in 45 minutes?* And so I'd argue, give him a bit back. A classic dressing room ding-dong, set to repeat.

Eventually, I began to realise what Dave was doing. He was singling me out because he knew I could take it. He could go mad at me and, being the laid-back and self-confident person I was, I'd trot back on to the pitch totally unaffected. Despite his verbal battering, my head wouldn't go down. He targeted me specifically because I was one of the biggest characters in the dressing room. Instead of going for somebody else who'd wilt in the face of the onslaught, he came for me. Dave was part manager, part psychologist. He knew that other players would look at him tearing into me and think, *Hang on! If he can talk to Michail like that, what's he going to do to me? I'd better lift it in the second half or I'm going to be in the shit here.* Yes, Dave was talking (very loudly) to me, but he was talking to everybody. It's a clever way of lifting your team, so long as you pick the right person. And in Dave's case that was yours truly. Every week I'd be there – 'I am f***ing running! Can't you see?' It would drive me mad. But equally, no matter how many times he ripped the shit out of me, by the end of the game it was all forgotten. 'Well done, Michail! Great stuff!'

That was the thing with me and Dave. Neither of us ever held a grudge. I had so many arguments with him, not just during games but in training. I could tell him to his face, in front of all the boys, 'You can f*** off!', and half an hour later we'd be chatting away, joking even, like nothing had happened. Totally back to normal. We believed in the value of, 'If there's something to be said, say it!' That approach worked for both of us. If either of us felt frustrated, we knew we could have it out and there'd be zero resentment left inside. We'd dealt with it and that was that. Another player might sit in his corner while a manager's going off on one, quietly nodding his head, and on the inside be disagreeing with every word that's being said. They might not feel they have a voice, or they might lack the confidence to speak up for themselves. They'll leave that room annoyed because they couldn't summon up the willpower to defend themselves. There are so many players like that, but I've never been one of them. I'm a person who will make myself heard. If you annoy me or if I feel you're not treating me right, I will let you know. And if I see the same thing happening to a friend, I will step in and stand up for them too. I have to be like that. Otherwise, I'd have all kinds of emotions fizzing inside. I wouldn't be able to focus on my game, or my life.

I always wanted a good relationship with my manager. I wanted to have that freedom to ask where I needed to make improvements or, if I'd struggled in a game, where I'd gone wrong. Why wouldn't I? The manager is the most important person to any footballer. All that matters is whose name is on the team sheet, and 90 per cent of the time that is me. Equally, if I feel like I should be playing, or that I'm not being treated fairly, I will let my manager know. I'm quite a laidback character in everything in life – except football. I've had to fight for so much in my career. Rolling over and letting someone dictate my future isn't in my personality. In football, I've found that being open and honest is the route to better relationships, especially with older managers. When players hold grudges, bitterness builds and builds. That dam will burst eventually and anger flood out in a way that's going to damage all concerned: player, manager, club and team. Much better to be honest from the start.

There was another reason me and Dave could tear strips off each other. We were cut from the same cloth. Yes, he was the manager and I was the player, but we both had exactly the same attitude. 'Get out there and get the job done!' There was a mutual respect, a recognition that we needed each other. I needed him to play me, and he needed me to do well. In many ways, of all the managers I had, Dave helped me the most. He made me the number nine, kept me in the team, and in return I just kept scoring goals. We were a good combination – with the occasional eruption! Not that I'd want to give the impression I was the only one on the end of Dave's explosive bollockings. He could properly rip the place up. He'd be in people's faces, his trademark line, 'It's not f***ing good enough!' bouncing off the walls of the dressing room. While not quite in the class of Sir Alex Ferguson, who once, infamously, kicked a boot at David Beckham, Dave wasn't averse to putting his foot through anything that happened to be in front of him – water bottle or whatever – when the rage struck. That might sound a bit over the top, but if I'm honest, players respond to managers going ballistic.

Old-school gaffers like Neil Warnock are looked on as dinosaurs now, but the way they operated worked. Much better to get something out in the open and deal with it. Don't allow whatever the problem is to fester and become poisonous within the changing room, or worse, in public. It feels like every week you see players throwing shirts or snubbing the gaffer when they're subbed off. No matter how pissed off I am, I've never lost it with a manager in front of the crowd or the cameras. You might see the frustration in my face, but I've never shouted, 'For f***'s sake!' or thrown a shirt or a bottle. In public, I prefer to keep my annoyance to myself. That's not to say I'm hunky-dory with the situation. It's not the best feeling to be subbed off, especially when you feel like you're doing all right. In fact, even when that's not the case, you're still desperate to stay on. But sometimes you have to rein in your ego. Everyone in football thinks they're the best, and you're no different. You still think there's something you can do to get yourself into the game. But there'll always be times when the manager sees things differently. 'Nah, your time is up.'

People say the best bosses are those who man-manage, who put an arm around one player to encourage them while giving another a gentle kick up the arse. I'll be honest, if those kinds of touchy-feely managers exist, I haven't really come across them. Far from it. Down the years I've seen managers smack things off tables, punch whiteboards, the lot. You might wonder if all this shouting and bawling can ever actually change anything, especially within a few minutes at half-time, but it obviously does. Firing people up, getting the boys to understand exactly what's wanted from them, is massive. That's why a team can be trailing 2–0 at the interval and still come back to win 3–2. Half-time is the key opportunity for a manager to get as much information as possible back on to the pitch. He can bellow from the touchline all he wants during the match, but the chances of his players hearing him above the crowd are minimal. A boss has to get his message across, quickly and impactfully, to everyone, whatever their age, whatever their character. As a younger player, you might not be listening too hard in the dressing room. Recovering after a hard-fought 45 minutes, it's all too easy to sit there in your own little daydream. As you get older and more mature you begin to realise that what's said in the break is so important, and the manager has to reach everyone. If that means a bit of drama, so be it. A good boss will also mix it up. As well as the loud stuff, perhaps aimed at a few key individuals, and a few important messages passed on to the team in general, if he's identified something a player can do better or more effectively, he'll find time to speak to them one on one. 'OK, Michail, this is what you need to do.'

Over the course of my career, I've seen shouting matches in the dressing room become less and less frequent. The difference between then and now is stark. They used to happen regularly, but while managers could once have a full-blown argument with a footballer and the next day everything be fine, today if a manager shouts at a player, chances are they'll down tools and refuse to play for them. They'll accuse them of being disrespectful. That element of 'Have a go at me and I'll have a go at you' has pretty much disappeared. Everything's a lot more delicately balanced now. Footballers are so much more precious. Managers simply haven't got the authority to talk to them like they might have done in the past, and so they tip-toe around. But who benefits in that scenario? The manager isn't getting what they really want from the player, while the player potentially doesn't perform as effectively as they might if the manager was brutally honest about what they could be doing better.

I get that the game has changed. It's got faster, techniques have improved and everyone's playing better football, but there's still room for a happy medium between old attitudes and new. Like I say, there was never any frustration in mine and David Moyes' relationship because we always voiced exactly what we wanted from each other, although even Dave slowly had to adapt to the new way of behaving around the modern footballer. That's why, to my mind anyway, he was a better manager at West Ham first time round. During that initial period, when he was brought in on a short-term contract to firefight possible relegation, he said it how it was. When he returned, putting down roots at the club for more than four years, he gradually lost that in-your-face element. I'm not saying he was bad during his second spell, that was when we won the Europa Conference League after all, I just think if he'd been his old explosive self we'd have done better in the other competitions as well. Instead, it felt like he'd tried to adapt himself to the times. Football in general was starting to get a bit softer, managers who ranted and raved were increasingly seen as relics of another age, and he responded by being much quieter and more in his shell. In some ways I felt for him. Management now is a headache. There's a lot of big egos in the game and dealing with that isn't easy. At a football club, you'll have 25 players. That's 25 egos. You can guarantee every single one of those players will think they're the best in their position. For a manager, that's difficult. It's up to them to keep a lid on any simmering resentment. Telling a player to sit on the bench and suck it up won't wash anymore. A modern manager needs to know about modern footballers – and that means being a tightrope walker.

A lot of people think it's just British managers who have an inbuilt ability to go up like a rocket on bonfire night. But don't let appearances be deceptive. Just because a lot of the overseas guys look like university professors doesn't mean they behave like them. They'll try their very best not to, but they're more than capable of losing their shit too. In fact, of all my West Ham managers, the only one who didn't really lose his shit, at least according to my friends in the dressing room (I didn't spend that much time in his company – of which more later) was actually British, Graham Potter.

But Dave was the one whose personality most resonated with me – that ability, if necessary, to lose it, but also to understand and communicate to his team as people as well as professionals.

Contrast that with the manager next through the door at West Ham after Dave's first term. I never had more issues with a boss than I did with Manuel Pellegrini. I found myself in a nightmarish situation with the Chilean, really struggling to understand what the hell was going on. As a footballer I always believed in, 'Play well, get your rewards. Don't play well, get your punishments.' But under Pellegrini that went totally out of the window. I never knew where I stood. I'd start one week, do well, maybe even be the best player on the pitch, and then the following week I wouldn't be in the starting 11. Worse, not even on the bench. I'd look at the team sheet and barely be able to believe what I was seeing. *What the …? How am I not on there?* If I'd underperformed, had two or three bad games, I could understand, but to be left out on the back of games where I'd shone? There was one time when we'd played one of the top six clubs away from home. I thought I'd had a great game, and then, the week after, Pellegrini pulled me aside. 'You're not in the squad tomorrow.' I started laughing. Genuinely, I thought it was a joke. He looked straight at me. 'No, no, Mikey, you're actually not.' I just couldn't believe it.

Pellegrini's style was to chop and change players a lot, but I was getting left out of the squad more than others. Humiliatingly, sometimes I'd start a game only to be subbed off at half-time or early after the restart. There were times when I didn't know whether I was coming or going, and that constant insecurity, zero stability, really affected me, driving me further and further down. That negative mental state was counter to everything I considered myself to be. I'm a positive person. I try to stay upbeat. If there's a problem, I'll find a way through it. But this was something else. It was like I had no control whatsoever over what was happening to me. I mean, I get it. If you don't perform, you get dropped and have to wait for an opportunity to reestablish yourself in the team. But Pellegrini? His approach made no sense at all.

In these kinds of situations some players will talk to teammates, try to get their frustration off their chest that way. But I didn't want to look like I was going round bitching behind the gaffer's back. And anyway, why would I talk to a player? They couldn't change anything. The manager was the only person who could do that. At one stage I found myself actually lying in bed crying. Through the tears streaming down my face, I found myself saying words I never thought possible. 'I think I might need to retire. I don't know if I can keep doing this. I don't know if I can handle it.' That might sound a bit over the top, but I meant it. Happiness is everything to me. If ever I've felt dejected, my way has always been to change direction, look for joy elsewhere. Life's too short to spend your time doing things that bring you down. If a situation is in your power to change, then change it. Retiring was the way of changing it. I knew West Ham wouldn't sell me, so instead I'd just call it a day at the age of 29. My wife was doing her best to console me. 'If you really want to quit, then you can. It's up to you. You don't have to be unhappy.' My sister, agent and brother also talked it through with me, and in the end, I was able to keep going. Fortunately so, because not long after, it was like something switched in Pellegrini's head. The side was struggling and he started using me. From then on, I was one of the first names on the team sheet.

There was something else Pellegrini did that's guaranteed to piss footballers off – criticise his players in public. After one game against Manchester City, he told the media I'd had two chances that I 'must score'. I wasn't surprised. And to be honest, I probably should have scored those opportunities, so maybe he had the right to say what he did, but, other than potentially pissing one of his players off, it's still hard to work out what he was trying to achieve by doing so. It wasn't like I could go back out on the pitch and try again.

I watch a lot of football and see managers make this public criticism mistake again and again. After just his third game in charge of Rangers, for instance, Russell Martin chose to use a post-match interview after another desperate result to publicly lambast his players. A lot of the time, managers slag off the team to appeal to the fans. 'I've seen what you've seen, and I'm not happy with it.' In so doing they're also taking some of the onus away from themselves. 'It's not my fault. I told the players to play a certain way and they didn't do it.' Their tactics haven't worked on the pitch and so now, off the pitch, they've employed a new one – deflection. But, as a former player himself, Martin should have known how damaging it can be to team spirit to air your dirty laundry in public. It annoyed me as a player, and it still annoys me now. One thing I grew up with, and always accepted, and believed is right, is that what a manager says in the changing room should stay in the changing room. Go in there and absolutely rip the shit out of every single player if you want, but when you then step out in front of the media defend your players to the hilt. It works exactly the same the other way round. Despite the performance, whatever player is sent out in front of the cameras defends the manager. A team must have a united front. It can never be players versus manager or vice-versa. That's completely wrong. The minute you do that, there's division. And once there's division, nothing's going to work. The manager wants the players to do as he asks, but they don't like him, so how's that going to happen? It's a long way back from there. Too far usually. Russell Martin never got Rangers going and was sacked not long after.

Managers really should take a leaf out of David Moyes' book and learn which players they can tear into and who they can't. Not everyone is going to be able to deal with the boss blaming them, and even fewer will thank him for doing so in front of the media. Ripping players that way can only be a recipe for disaster. It opens the door for journalists to start asking the players whether they thought the manager was right in his assessment. As I say, a player should defend his manager, but now, after his boss's little outburst, if a player says the gaffer was wrong, that it was actually the tactics that were to blame, who's the manager to complain? He's the one who started mouthing off. The best teams are those where everyone pulls together and protects each other. You never see good managers dissing the dressing room in front of the media. Their approach is clear. 'I'm the one in charge and it's down to me to get these players to perform the way I want them to. Give me the shit, not them.'

I never had it out with Pellegrini about any of his decisions that affected me. I wouldn't say he was unapproachable, but I could see there was absolutely no point. He wasn't going to let what a player said influence him. I also felt that going to the gaffer and saying, 'I can't handle how you're treating me' would make me seem weak. I didn't want to give anyone, let alone a manager, that hold over me. If I bumped into Pellegrini now, however, it's definitely something I'd ask him about. Why was that his philosophy? Why did he feel like continually leaving players out was a good way of getting the best out of them? I'd love some kind of understanding of what his reasoning was, same as I'd like him to comprehend how unpredictable selection decisions and lack of communication affect players' morale and mental health. Pellegrini was the biggest illustration I ever had of a key point about being a footballer – the power is never in your hands. Usually, football's pretty simple. Keep performing and you keep playing. With Pellegrini that went out the window. Whatever authority I thought I had over my destiny was removed. And it hurt like mad.

In the end, Pellegrini was the biggest dressing room bust-up I never had. Shame really, as when I blow, I really do blow! Just ask my first West Ham manager, Slaven Bilić. Eventually, Slaven would be unbelievable for me, but at first he didn't really want to play me, mainly because he didn't want me at Upton Park in the first place. My agent had a good relationship with the Hammers and sent the chairman David Sullivan a video. 'Let's give him a go,' was his reaction, and next thing I knew I was through the door.

It's weird when you're brought in by the owner rather than the manager. It's a whole other level of trying to prove yourself. I wasn't Slaven's signing and he wasn't really feeling me. To be fair, why would he? Other than me being a winger who could score a few goals, he didn't know anything about me. While I was doing well in training, showing what I was about, his signing was Victor Moses, on loan from Chelsea. Even so, a couple of weeks later I made my debut. That first game was a real baptism of fire, away at Manchester City. With half-an-hour left and us unexpectedly winning 2–1, Slaven brought me on to bolster the left side of defence. That's what you call a test – at the Etihad with the home team desperately pushing for a goal. Naturally, we were pinned in our own half for pretty much the whole time. But I didn't do anything wrong. I wasn't nervous about playing at that level and helped the team hold out for a famous win against the odds. My reward? I didn't touch the pitch again for three months. It became a running joke, 'Michail the laminate' other players called me, because I never moved off the bench. That didn't piss me off. Why would it? It was a fact and I saw the humorous side. But the funniest moment of all came when a fan tweeted the club's co-chairman David Gold with a picture of me. 'Please RT,' the post read, 'trying to raise awareness for my mate who went missing in Manchester a few weeks ago.' David, not realising what the fan was referring to, only went and retweeted it! I had a good laugh about that. To be fair, David, who died in 2023, was 79 at the time and probably not the best on social media.

Going into any club as the chairman's buy is always going to be tricky. The manager doesn't want you and so it follows that you're going to be on the fringes of the squad. You arrive on that first day thinking, *Oh my God, am I going to even play?* In my case, I did play and then was left to twiddle my thumbs on the sidelines. There was even talk of me going out on loan, but no way was that happening. My attitude was simple. *I'm not going back to the Championship. I'm in the Premier League and I'm here to do a job.* What got me through that period was self-belief. I knew I could make Slaven understand what I could bring to his team. And he did come to see exactly that – unfortunately, it was in a position completely alien to me. If I was going to be a regular in his team, it would have to be as right-back. Considering my favoured position is left-wing I wasn't exactly keen, but West Ham had a load of injuries in defence and needed someone to fill the gap. I told myself that playing in the Premier League was what I'd always wanted and now I'd been handed the opportunity to go out and show what I could do, even if it was in a role I was totally unfamiliar with. To say it was a big shift would be the understatement of the century. Aside from those few minutes against Manchester City I had, quite literally, never played defensively in my entire life. Suddenly my whole world was about running backwards instead of forwards. That takes time to get used to. And time's the last thing you have in the Premier League.

Thrown in at the deep end, my way of surviving was to play right-back in a way I recognised – as a winger. I was knocking the ball down the line, getting crosses in. I did all that and the defensive stuff as well. And I wasn't bad at it. My attitude as a defender was that no-one was going to beat me; no way was that going to happen. Of course, some players are different class, especially Eden Hazard. He'd get the ball and just drive infield. The second he did that I was chasing shadows. Hazard aside, however, by the end of the season I'd played more than two-thirds of the games and got eight goals, which from defence is pretty good by anybody's standards. Guys who can contribute like that are pretty rare, and clearly Slaven knew that better than anyone. He sold our defender James Tomkins and told me he wanted me to be his number one. I got why Slaven wanted to convert me. I was quick, I was strong and I could score goals. I was good at right-back, so good that I even had top-four clubs looking at me.

'I can make you one of the best right-backs in Europe,' Slaven told me. I understood my potential in that position, and moving to a top-four club would have meant big money, but my attitude was, *Do I really want to go through my career playing for finances?* Because that's what would have happened. I mean, what price do you put on your own happiness? Maybe I'm someone who makes decisions that a lot of other people wouldn't. But I've always been the type who wants to push myself on my own terms. I made it as clear as I could.

'I really don't want to play there.'

'Trust me,' Slaven told me.

But I hated it. I wanted to be the player I always believed I could be.

GOOD BOSS, BAD BOSS

I played football because I enjoyed it. I just loved having the ball at my feet, running around and scoring goals. And so being a right-back just wasn't doing it for me. Towards the end of that season, one game more than any other made me realise I couldn't carry on. West Ham were playing Watford at home. We were 3–0 up after 53 minutes – and that was when the manager told me, 'Stay there! Behind the halfway line! Do not concede!' I'm looking up, there's Dimitri Payet (the best player I ever played with), Manuel Lanzini, all these boys running around having the best time, and I'm just stood there. I honestly felt like I was watching the game from the crowd. I'd been wanting to play in the Premier League my entire life. I'd got the opportunity, but in a position I hated. Enjoying football had always been my fuel and now someone had pulled the plug. I was so upset back in the dressing room. While usually I'd celebrate with the boys, right now all I wanted to do was shower and go home.

That was the day when I decided I couldn't do that job for Slaven anymore. I just couldn't be a right-back for the rest of my career. The situation reached a head in the very first game of the following season, against Chelsea at Stamford Bridge. Again, Slaven had me at right-back. I'm not going to lie, I made a massive mistake. I won the ball in our box, tried to dink it over Eden Hazard (him again!), made a mess of it, and in the chaos that followed tripped Hazard up and gave away a penalty. It showed exactly why right-back wasn't the best position for me. My attacking mindset had led directly to a mistake that contributed to us losing the match. Five minutes later, Slaven hooked me even though the second half had barely started. I spent the rest of the game on the bench quietly fuming.

After the final whistle, Slaven stormed into the dressing room. He made straight for me. 'I know you don't want to play at right-back,' he bellowed in a voice that could be heard halfway down the King's Road. 'People don't want to play here. People don't want to play there. But at the end of the day if I put you somewhere, you play there.'

His rage was hardly unexpected. But if he thought I was going to shrink under the onslaught, he was very much mistaken. OK, I'd made a mistake. But I'd done so while playing in a position that I'd said repeatedly wasn't where I was meant to be.

'I told you I didn't want to play there,' I came back at him. 'And I'm telling you right now, I'll never play there again. I'd rather be on the bench than do that. It's up to you. Either play me on the f***ing wing or don't play me at all.'

Even by the standards of dressing room set-tos this was clearly getting a little out of hand, and club captain Mark Noble and 'Ginge' wasted no time entering the fray. 'Who the f*** do you think you are?' they were asking me. 'You can't talk to him like that!' I stood up to them. 'F*** off! I'll say what I f***ing like!' A few of the other boys got in between us, but in the end I just walked away, straight out of the ground and into a taxi home.

The following week, Slaven played me at right-wing. I scored the first goal at the London Stadium in a 1–0 win against Bournemouth. For him to take on board what I was telling him and play me somewhere else was quite something.

It takes a big man to do what he did. He could easily have felt that I'd humiliated him in front of the dressing room. I'm sure a lot of managers would have taken it as a sign of disrespect. 'That's it, I'm done with this guy. He's not going to play for me ever again.' But Slaven's reaction was, 'All right, you know what? I'm going to give you what you want and see what you can do.' He gave me the opportunity, and I grabbed it with both hands. For the next nine seasons, aside from filling in at the back a couple of times, I played as the attacking player I truly was.

I'm not saying everyone should get into a confrontation with their manager (although it is quite entertaining if you're just sat there watching!) but long-term satisfaction as a footballer can only come from being true to yourself. I learned very early on that in football anything can change at any time. You're constantly being asked to adapt. Remembering who you are and what you're about is all that keeps you sane. Holding on to who you are and what you believe in is vital, because football is a machine which you have no control over. It moves forward relentlessly, swallowing everything in its path.

It can, and it will, eat you up and spit you out at any moment.

FIVE

THE CHASE FOR SUCCESS

It's a couple of days out from matchday. It's a big one – Manchester City.

The level of detail accorded to each and every game gets bigger every year – the in-club analysis is incredible – and the management has sat us down to take us through exactly what they want. What follows is a full breakdown of exactly how City play, how each player fits into the pattern, what they're trying to achieve, how we can stop them doing it and how we can exploit certain elements of their set-up for ourselves. The intricacy of the plans, the exact requirements for each player in the room and the absolute necessity to implement them on the day, makes for a pretty intense atmosphere. Essentially, we sit there, listen and hope it all goes in.

Problem is these talks always happen in very warm rooms with the lights down for the projector. It's not uncommon to start panicking a bit inside.

Oh no, I could easily nod off here!
I look up, trying to refocus, desperate to keep
awake. My eyes fall on Manuel Pellegrini's right-hand
man Rubén Cousillas. He's fast asleep. Again.

For football managers, the only guarantee is the sack. And with more and more owners demanding instant success, the managerial merry-go-round spins faster and faster every year. Then again, one thing you soon learn as a professional footballer is that the game moves quickly. Very quickly. Look at my ten years at West Ham. In that time the club went through Slaven Bilić, David Moyes (twice), Manuel Pellegrini, Julen Lopetegui and Graham Potter. Six managerial changes in a decade – and compared to some clubs that's not even particularly bad.

Nottingham Forest is a great example. When I joined them in August 2014, they were already on their 12th manager of the 2000s. That man was Stuart Pearce, an absolute legend at the club, playing more than 500 games and winning two League Cups along the way. Famous for his fierce determination and even fiercer tackles, Stuart was known to fans of Forest and England simply as Psycho. But Stuart the manager was completely different to Stuart the footballer. He was actually pretty quiet, never really lost it, and spoke to his players respectfully. He was a hard-working coach just getting on doing his job. I really got along with Stuart and felt bad for him when the team stopped winning. We had a blistering start, unbeaten after 11 league games, but injuries to Chris Cohen and Andy Reid destroyed our midfield and left us with just three wins from the next 17 fixtures. It wasn't like Stuart could just wave a magic wand and replace two influential midfielders. What went wrong was his attempt to use other players in the same role rather than adapt to the situation he found himself in. And so 12 became 13. In February, Stuart was replaced by another former Forest man, Dougie Freedman, who steadied the ship and saw us to a lower mid-table finish. Dougie was a bit more unpredictable compared to Stuart. He could properly lose it, and yet at other times be the calmest person around. While eventually things turned sour with Dougie, what both he and Stuart did was allow me to play with freedom, which meant I felt secure despite the change of manager halfway through the season.

People often wonder if it affects players when there's speculation that their manager is going to get the boot. I can tell you right now it doesn't. It might be a manager the players like, it might be the complete opposite, it makes no difference. If it's happening, it's happening. There's nothing we can do about it and that's the end of it. Forget the manager's job, what we have to do is focus on our own. Let's face it, he's getting sacked because we're not performing on the pitch. Part of that might be down to him not getting his tactics right, but we still need to do our job. I also get asked more and more if Premier League clubs are sacking managers too quickly. My answer's always the same – football's increasingly a results sport, and if they're not coming then any boss is under threat. The luxury of being allowed to bed-in simply isn't there like it used to be.

Some managers do come in and turn things round just like that. Often that's no coincidence. It's inevitable that, with a new boss through the door, the players start working that little bit harder. The boys who are already in the starting line-up want to stay there. Those who aren't will be doing their very best to impress. For them, a new manager offers a great opportunity to show what they can do and force their way into the side. That's why, nine times out of ten, when a new gaffer comes in you get a bounce, because at that point everybody, the entire squad, raises their level.

And yet others come along with a great reputation and can't win a game. Forget new-manager bounce, they can't get the team off the floor. Often that's because they're trying to do too much too quickly. A clever manager will come in, get to know the team, understand the philosophy they've been playing with and then work with those players to turn things round. What they won't do is impose their own philosophy on a side which might not have the personnel to carry it out. Look at Ange Postecoglou when he took over the Nottingham Forest hotseat early in the 2025–26 season. After losing his first game 3–0 at Arsenal, he told everyone they'd see his imprint on the team by the time of their Carabao Cup tie at Swansea four days later. 'It won't be months, it won't be weeks, it'll be Wednesday.' The minute he said that, he was in trouble. Not only did he put a load of unnecessary pressure on himself but there was no way that big a transformation could happen successfully in such a short space of time. Why make it so much about himself? Go in there, keep your head down, get to know the players and adapt slowly.

I understand that managers have philosophies. But unless they understand, *really* understand, the nature of the players and the club they're working with, they're going to get sacked. I honestly feel that Graham Potter could be a good manager – at the right club with the right players. At West Ham, he saw an opportunity. He got himself a good wage and a good team. But what type of team was it? Expansive? Or one that needed to be narrow and counterattack? Potter tried to create an expansive side when he should have done the exact opposite. At that point West Ham had some brilliant playmakers, well capable of finding a good fast pass and putting someone through on goal. Every time West Ham have succeeded in recent times, that's what they've done. Look at David Moyes. Both times he managed the club we played narrow. It was all about putting players in behind and scoring goals. Slaven was the same. We played good, dogged football, and it worked. So Potter coming in and trying to get the boys playing pretty football was never going to be a success. For a long time now, West Ham have been an ugly team that needs to play ugly football. The club probably wouldn't wish to describe itself as such, but that's the reality. It's all very well to say, 'We need a change of style. We want more possession of the ball.' No. What you need is wins.

At the same time, whenever a new manager comes in, players want to give him a chance. After all, he's the one picking the team, and, you never know, his ideas could work. The only way to find out is by doing what he wants. If it doesn't work out, then obviously it's back over to the chairman to make another decision.

Ultimately, achievement feeds off positivity. Players need to work for one another and so a good manager will foster unity in the camp. If a team is going to succeed, togetherness is critical. David Moyes was particularly good at constructing the kind of squad where not only would everyone work for each other, they'd fight for each other. He'd build team spirit by taking the boys away for a few days or putting on social events which included their partners. Say what you like about Dave and his style of football, but in any squad he managed, there was always great camaraderie among the group. He knew that the bond within a team is every bit as important as any other ingredient in the recipe for success. It's precisely that spirit which will carry the players through to the other side when, as happens to every team, the going gets tough. Brendan Rodgers was the same when he was my manager at Reading, taking us go-karting and stuff. He didn't do that because it was a way to fill a quiet afternoon, a nice little jolly. He did it because he wanted a team rather than a bunch of individuals. Players see more of each other than we do our families. We don't need to be best mates, but as a team we do need to act as one.

It was exactly that unity which allowed that quality West Ham side of the early 2020s to pick itself up from one of its lowest moments and work towards its greatest. We all had a genuine belief that we'd win the Europa League in 2022. We absolutely thought that was going to happen. So, when we lost to Eintracht Frankfurt in the semi-final it hurt. I mean *really* hurt. Players were crying in the dressing room. Losing a massive game, especially one which offers what might be a once-in-a-lifetime chance to reach a European final, is like being punched in the heart. But we had to stick together and push on with the next challenge, finishing high enough in the Premier League to potentially secure a Champions League spot for the following season – a place that would have been guaranteed had we won the Europa League. That meant, after the crushing low of the Thursday, we had to be back on it at Norwich on the Sunday. No half measures. No licking our wounds. We had to perform. And we did. We won that game 4–0, and then held Manchester City the week after, before slipping to defeat in the last game of the season at Brighton and ending up in the Europa Conference League which, of course, we went on to win. By the time the final whistle went on the south coast, the team had played 56 games. Togetherness carried us to the end of that season. After every setback, we regrouped. We trusted in the manager, the staff and ourselves. We knew what we were doing was right.

The importance of unity raises the question of what happens in the dressing room when a player goes 'rogue' and ends up falling out with the club. Mo Salah's dispute with Liverpool at the end of 2025 is a great example. I heard pundits saying it was disruptive, that other players wouldn't be happy with what he'd done. But, having spent half my life in a dressing room I know that's not actually true. There's a universal truth to life as a footballer – one day you'll be cast aside. That being the case, no-one's going to criticise a team-mate for looking out for themselves. The problem only comes if that player isn't performing. If he's not out there on the pitch fighting alongside his teammates, there'll be resentment. Salah, however, didn't lack fight. He just wasn't having a good season, which is an entirely different matter.

We had a bit of a 'Salah' situation with Dimitri Payet at West Ham. While he was seeking a move back to France, the club refused to sell. Frustrated and trying to force the issue, Dimitri wouldn't train or play which in turn affected how the fans thought of the Frenchman, who up to that point had been a bit of a legend. But there was no issue between him and the boys. We didn't dislike him. He wanted to move back to France and we had no problem with that. 'He wants to go – let him.' OK, he could have made his point in a slightly better way, maybe a little bit less disruptive, but it was no big deal. And that will have been the same with Salah at Liverpool. From the outside, it might look like a player is being selfish, complaining about their situation when it looks for all the world that they've got everything they could ever possibly want, but in that dressing room we understand that we have to stand up for ourselves.

These days you'll find leadership groups in a lot of dressing rooms. They help to drive an understanding of what standards are expected of the team. They also enable communication between the players and the boss. Fact is, when it comes to the day-to-day business of the team, the players know best. The manager doesn't know what's going on in the changing room for the simple reason that he's hardly ever in it. He spends most of his time in his office. But the players live in each other's pockets. For the same reason it's important that the captain isn't picked by the manager. If that happens there's a chance it won't be the right person, which can cause problems in itself. A big part of the captain's role is as a trusted bridge between players and management. If he's the gaffer's choice, then that trust is immediately compromised. A good manager will listen to his players, see them as people as well as footballers. Slaven Bilić was good at that. He genuinely cared about the boys and their families, their work/life balance. I've heard it said that he was too soft on some players, which backfired on him, but Slaven's problem came from his backroom staff who just weren't good enough to help him create lasting success.

I've been lucky in that, right from the start, I've clicked with a lot of my managers. Early on in my career, especially, I came across people who saw something in me and wanted to help me reach my potential. For all the big-name bosses I've played under, I'll always count Nigel Gibbs, assistant to Steve Coppell at Reading, as one of the biggest influences in my career. Training would start at 10.30, but Nigel would take me out half an hour earlier to work on my technique, finishing and crossing. 'Now you're here,' he told me, 'you need to work harder than every player already in the building. They've all had a headstart on you. They've all been to academies, had the extra training, had all the stuff you didn't have. You're here because of your natural ability, your rawness, but now you need to catch up on all the skills they've been working on for the last nine or 10 years.' I love Nigel. The effort he put into me is one of the biggest reasons I made it as a pro. I cannot thank him enough.

Martin Allen at Cheltenham Town is another whose advice and friendship I treasured. The former QPR and West Ham midfielder really did look after me – a manager, yes, but in many ways also a father figure. Like Nigel, Martin was always there, helping me out and encouraging me to come in early and do extra work on my technique and touch. At the time I didn't have a car, which is where Martin would go above and beyond, often driving me back home to London after a game. One time I asked him to drop me off at Tooting & Mitcham FC where my family had hired the function room for a party. Except he didn't drop me off. He parked up and came right in to say hello, shaking everyone's hands and chatting to them. As a young player making his way, that meant a lot to me, like he cared about me as a person rather than simply a player. Gestures like that, which went beyond the pitch, gave me a sense of belonging and confidence.

In Alan Pardew at Southampton, again I found someone who not only believed in me but gave me valuable insight into what was needed to thrive as a pro. In Alan's case that was consistency. Most footballers, even in the lower leagues, have quality and technique, but it's performing consistently that singles a player out. Having previously managed in the Premier League with Charlton and West Ham, Alan knew what was required if I was to reach that level. At that point in my career, he pointed out, I was putting in a great perform-ance, a nine out of ten, one week, only for my level to dip next time out. 'Reliability,' he told me, 'is what you need.' In the Prem, he explained, that meant being a minimum seven out of ten week after week. Alan was also incredibly laid-back and so gave players the freedom to control their own lives. He made you feel like you were an adult, capable of making decisions, whereas some managers seem to think that they need to treat you like a kid.

What all those early managers gave me was an understanding – the value of each cross, each individual action, and the importance of playing to a high standard over a long period. Facing the challenges they put in front of me, such as adapting to new tactical expectations, or unfamiliar training routines, was a big part of the growth process that eventually got me the opportunity at West Ham.

What I then had to deal with was the churn of managers within a single club. It's that thing about 'philosophy' again. Every manager who comes in brings a different one with them. Manuel Pellegrini has a completely different approach to David Moyes, same as Slaven Bilić does to Graham Potter. If you don't fit into that plan, then chances are you're on your way. Because I'm a raw player, not the prettiest, I had a tough time with every new West Ham manager, always having to convince them what I could do. They'd come in with a strategy and see me as not fitting into it. What generally happened then was that things wouldn't go particularly well, their style wouldn't produce results and they'd resort to more direct play. Suddenly I was flavour of the month! I could get the ball where it needed to be and make something happen. I'd get a cross into the box, score a goal. Looking pretty is all very well but it has to get you somewhere. My touch might not be the best, I might not be the most technical of players, but that doesn't always matter. It doesn't mean you're not effective. While constantly having to prove myself wasn't ideal, it did help me as a footballer because I was always stretching myself, showing manager after manager what I could do.

The last time my West Ham manager changed I was in hospital after my car crash. I never got that opportunity to really show Julen Lopetegui what I could do. It actually took me a few weeks to tell myself that wasn't important. All that mattered was getting back to fitness. Whatever the name on the manager's door, rush my recovery and I wouldn't be able to display to the full degree what I could do.

More than any other manager, Gareth Southgate is held up as the one who really did treat footballers like humans, not robots, and from my own brief flirtation with the national team I could see it was a reputation entirely justified. The first time I went to St George's Park, home to the National Football Centre, I was struck by how barren it was. Stuck outside Burton-on-Trent, it was quite horrendous, like a luxury prison. Other than a Starbucks, there was just nowhere to go. It was exactly the sort of unstimulating environment in which players could well retreat to their rooms and spend their free time on their phones or PlayStations. Gareth immediately saw that was a problem. Ever the innovator, he brought in things like golf simulators and a basketball court. He saw the importance of the squad spending bonding time with each other. And it was precisely the right approach.

That first time I joined up with England, players were spending a lot of time away from one another. The team spirit that only comes from understanding what makes one another tick was lacking. Steven Gerrard has said it himself – before Gareth came along England players were like strangers to each other, sticking tightly to their own little club factions, and it affected the England team. The 'golden generation' should have achieved, but they didn't, and the distance between the players, the cliques they formed, was a big reason why. Club rivalries got in the way of the bigger picture. Liverpool players didn't want to speak to Manchester United players. Chelsea players didn't want to speak to either. But if you're representing your country, you've got to have some kind of relationship. To succeed, togetherness needs to be the same as at your club. If someone gets kicked on the field, every teammate should be straight over there backing them up. I might not have been around his team as long as I'd have liked, but I could feel the vibe that Gareth was creating, how he was trying to get everyone to bond together, encouraging them to talk openly in front of one another, to open up about their experiences on and off the pitch. And look how it worked. He led England to the 2018 World Cup semi-final, and the final of Euro 2020 and 2024. An incredible turnaround for the national team after years of failure and disappointment.

The success of Gareth and other innovative leaders means management is changing. Whereas before it was a bit of a merry-go-round, the same faces getting all the jobs, now clubs are more willing to try something new, something fresh. People with less experience are not only coming in but doing well, bringing new methods with them – which all too often means trying to stay awake in those pre-match analysis meetings! So much in the modern game is worked out well in advance. There's a pattern of play for every eventuality. For instance, when a player's getting subbed on, you might notice a coach desperately thumbing through a folder, trying to find the right page to show them. It's a bit like watching someone flicking through the Argos catalogue, except in this case instead of washing machines and headphones it's full of set-piece routines. Some managers make the subs watch set-pieces so they'll know what to do if they come on. Others aren't so bothered. Either way, you can't have a player just wandering on and thinking, *OK, I'll stand over here.* Set-pieces are massive in the modern game. They offer a real opportunity to get the ball in the net. Players have to know where to be. And if that routine comes off, it's often the difference between the sides. We need to know all this set-piece stuff, combined with dozens of other snippets of tactical information. There's a myth that says footballers aren't always the cleverest of people, but the amount of information they carry in their head from game to game, implementing it as they go along, right there in the thick of the action, would suggest otherwise.

In the end, whatever the various managers' tactics or philosophies, some teams will succeed, others will slide into oblivion. One manager celebrating with his side at the end of the season, the other staring down the barrel of the chairman's gun. And, this being football, both facing, pretty much inevitably, the bullet in the end (and people wonder why I don't want to try it myself!).

Football is a sport where, for most clubs, most of the time, success is out of reach. The lows outnumber the highs. Which makes in itself for some pretty interesting situations ...

SIX
FANS

We're playing Burnley at home when out of the corner of my eye I see a West Ham fan on the pitch. What the f***'s going on here? He walks past me – and he doesn't look happy. In fact, he looks very pissed off. I get the feeling he hasn't entered the field of play to slap us on the back and tell us, 'Keep it up! Well played!'

I'm thinking, What do I even do? when club captain Mark Noble steps up and wrestles him to the ground. OK, this is turning into a very weird afternoon. I'm just getting my head round Nobes' intervention when another bloke appears. This guy's got something in his hand. It's a corner flag! Which he plants in the centre circle. What the actual f***?

No two ways about it, the place is absolutely boiling over.

That Burnley game, coming towards the end of the 2017–18 season, was massive for us, a classic relegation scrap, and one we desperately needed to win. We lost 3–0. The fans lost their heads. At one point they gathered in front of the directors' box. 'You destroyed our club!', 'Sack the board!' Plastic bottles, coins, all sorts, were being thrown. Co-chairmen David Gold and David Sullivan were forced to head inside for their own safety. At the end of the game, they had to stay in the ground to let the crowd disperse. The players were fine to leave. The fans, seriously unimpressed that West Ham were dicing with relegation less than two years after moving to the London Stadium, were after the owners, not us.

Playing for West Ham can be difficult. It's a crazy club. It's got a 62,000-seater stadium and 50,000 season ticket holders, and yet has traditionally struggled, both to compete with the other big London sides and to break through into the top six in the Premier League. That means, wearing the famous claret and blue, you need to know how to deal with the pressure of supporter expectation. Once you understand that, you soon realise you're playing for a club where the fanbase is unbelievable. Every single place I've been in the world I've met West Ham fans. Thailand, Gran Canaria, Los Angeles, you name it. I reckon I could be on top of Everest and I'd feel a tap on my shoulder. 'Michail! I'm a Hammers fan! All right mate?' The same goes for the support on the road. Whenever, wherever, the Hammers play, they're there, giving their all. Win or lose they always back the team in massive numbers. But until I joined them, I never realised quite how big the club is. While they might not have made that leap into the top six, it's not for want of trying. You can't argue with the fact that David Sullivan has ploughed a lot of money into West Ham. The problem a lot of the time is that his managers have wasted it. They've spent big, sometimes £45–50 million, on players only for them to totally underperform. That's a problem when other clubs are improving around you. Competition in the Premier League has never been more fierce. Year on year, teams are improving. The ever-increasing amount of money at their disposal means they can sign better and better players. Look at the strides Newcastle United have made in recruitment during the past few seasons.

Over long periods, one thing in West Ham's favour has been their consistency. While a lot of clubs have been relegated from the Prem and fallen away for quite a while, West Ham have enjoyed a presence at the top table. For fans, however, treading water is never good enough, which means there's often periods of discontent, and, naturally, the vast majority of it is aimed at the chairman. Fans often feel like the club is badly run and David Sullivan needs either to sell-up or do better. Sometimes you can see their point. When West Ham sold striker Mohammed Kudus to Tottenham, one of their biggest rivals, in the summer of 2025, it was obviously going to spark a massive amount of resentment. The club would argue that it needed the money. OK, but do you sell to your biggest Premier League rival? When it comes to fan relations, it's pretty much the worst thing you can do.

The move to the London Stadium, billed as the launchpad for West Ham to become one of the big boys, has been another hard sell. A lot of West Ham fans have never come to terms with leaving Upton Park. The London Stadium wasn't built for football, its purpose was to host the 2012 Olympics, and fans complain that the atmosphere is completely different. They're not wrong. At the old ground the crowd was so close to the pitch it felt like they were on top of us. The atmosphere was incredible and I'm glad I joined the club just in time to experience it before the bulldozers moved in at the end of the 2015–16 season. Funny how often big games happen at key times. The last match at Upton Park was under the floodlights against Man Utd, who the Hammers have had plenty of great battles with down the years. I've never known an atmosphere like that. An absolute one-off. Before we even got to the ground the roads were flooded with fans, many of them with faces painted claret and blue. A lot of them didn't have tickets. They just wanted to be in the vicinity of the stadium on such an historic night. The fact we came out on top, fighting back from 2–1 down to win 3–2, and I scored, just made it even more special. We did a lap of the ground afterwards, a real hairs-on-the-back-of-the-neck moment. All that history, 112 years in that famous old stadium. If it had to come to an end, then every West Ham fan couldn't have been happier it finished that way. The players were the same. We continued the celebrations back inside the dressing room, jumping in the ice-baths and Jacuzzis. The stars definitely aligned that night.

Often players and managers talk about the crowd being a 12th man. You might think they're hollow words, an easy way to get the supporters onside and make them feel involved, but in my experience that's right. On a practical level, noisy fans put pressure on the referee. Maybe that 50/50 decision goes your way. But more important is the lift they give the team. When things aren't quite happening, a sudden surge of support really does give you an extra push. West Ham had that advantage at Upton Park. Anfield felt the same. The Liverpool crowd is so loud, so behind their team, that the old cliché about them sucking the ball into the back of the net does feel true. The pressure of playing there as an away team is crazy. Everything you do has to be twice as good as normal or you'll suffer big-time. It's like you're pushing against a wall. Even the very best sides in the world feel it. Look at that amazing Champions League win over Barcelona in 2019 when the Reds overcame a 3–0 first-leg deficit to win 4–3. The Liverpool fans sniffed the possibility of a miracle. The atmosphere they created that night was electric and went a long way to making it happen.

Playing away from home at intimidating stadiums, managers will often encourage their team to stifle the opposition for the first 20 minutes and keep the supporters quiet. Get the crowd on the home team's backs and you create the kind of pressure that brings mistakes. As a player, there's nothing worse than hearing a collective groan when you misplace a pass or an opposition player gets past you. I've seen players react by completely losing their heads. Suddenly they're trying to pick out crazy passes, beat three men, in a desperate attempt to please the fans, whereas the correct thing to do is to stay professional, keep to the gameplan, and do what needs to be done. When an away team employs that tactic at a ground where there's already simmering unrest, as has happened on occasion at the London Stadium, it's amazing how often it pays dividends. There's a powder keg of frustration just sat there – and the away team can't wait for it to explode. Amid the carnage, they steal in and disappear with the three points. What's worse, every team in the league will see that happen and make it their business to create exactly the same negative atmosphere when they arrive. For the home team, it's an incredibly difficult spiral to escape from.

Maybe West Ham fans would have warmed to the new stadium a bit quicker had the club made more of an attempt to take the Boleyn Ground atmosphere with them. As a season-ticket holder you get to know everybody around you. You might have been sitting with them for decades. But no thought went into replicating that environment at the new ground. They just sold season tickets willy nilly. Instead of their old mates, fans found themselves sitting with strangers. Worse, some of them weren't even West Ham fans. They were just tourists wanting to see a game at a stadium they knew from the Olympics.

Today, while there's still the occasional banner protesting about the move, I do feel that the fans are getting more used to the London Stadium – because they've had to. It's not like Everton, who have kept Goodison Park for their women's team. The Boleyn Ground was reduced to rubble. These days it's flats. Our run to the final of the Europa Conference League also helped. There were some great nights at the stadium along the way. The protests came back when the club allowed the momentum from that brilliant achievement to fall away. West Ham fans have every right to want us to be right up there with the best and are not going to sit there meekly when it looks like their passion isn't being matched by the board. As a player, the unfortunate side to that is that while you might beat Man United, Chelsea and Tottenham all in a row, lose the next game to Burnley, Fulham, or Crystal Palace, and the frustration creeps back in. Forget the games you have won, suddenly all that matters is that one game you *should* have won. Suddenly you're back to being the worst team in the world. As a West Ham footballer, that kind of instant catastrophising is something you have to get used to. It's part and parcel of the job. West Ham had a terrible start to the 2025–26 season, losing 3–0 away to newly promoted Sunderland and then 5–1 to Chelsea at the London Stadium. Straight away all I was hearing from West Ham fans was doom and gloom. 'We're going down. The squad's not up to it.' I realise it wasn't exactly a blistering start, but that was after two games of the 38 that make up a Premier League season! Any team can have a bad start. It doesn't necessarily mean they're still going to be in the bottom three nine months later. Although, having said that …

When it comes to volatile crowds, the craziest thing I ever saw in a football ground came towards the end of West Ham's Europa Conference League semi-final second leg away at Dutch side AZ Alkmaar. Pablo Fornals scored our winning goal, cementing our place in the final, deep into injury time. I'd been subbed off shortly before, and, as the game resumed, all I could hear was a collective 'Ugh! Ugh! Ugh!' coming from the right of the dugouts. I looked round and saw a bunch of the home fans straining at the fence separating them from the main stand. When we scored, the players' families, sat in the executive seats, had jumped up and cheered. The Dutch fans thought there were West Ham supporters in an AZ Alkmaar area. Desperate to get in there to start a fight, with every yank of the fence they were making this 'Ugh!' sound. When they broke through and started to invade the stand, the West Ham players feared the worst. There were wives, girlfriends, mums, dads, all sorts in there. Flynn Downes saw his dad in the middle of the mayhem and leapt straight in. He wasn't alone. Jarrod Bowen was trying to get in there to help. Łukasz Fabiański too. In fact, quite a few boys had to jump in because it really did look like the trouble was going to get out of hand. I had no-one in there but still wanted to help. A security guard stopped me, but I could see it was total chaos – stewards, fans, fists flying, cops in riot gear. Anyone who had a loved-one in the middle of that lot had every right to be concerned. Thankfully, it was soon all brought under control, but it was a mad, mad, couple of minutes at the end of an unbelievable night.

I've been lucky enough to have had a good relationship with the fans wherever I've been in my career, but I've also been in teams that have struggled, which, of course, is when fans start to get restless and make their feelings known. One thing I've never really understood as a footballer is when fans claim, 'You're not playing for the badge!' Because, if you think about it, it's obvious we're not. None of us are. Unless we're a fan of that team, how can we be? I mean, how realistic is it to expect a player from Spain or Uruguay to be playing for a badge they might never have clapped eyes on before they were handed the shirt? Let's face it, if you turned up to an IT job and someone said, 'You need to work hard for that computer,' you'd be like, 'Shut up!' What we're playing for is something much bigger than the shirt. Professional pride is one part of it – we want to do well for ourselves and our teammates – but the overriding thing we're playing for is our livelihoods. At the end of the day, if we don't perform, we sink lower in the league and ultimately that means we get less money for ourselves and our families.

As much as fans might feel a player isn't playing for the shirt, he's definitely out there playing for himself, his children, his partner. No-one can tell me that the shirt is more important to a footballer than his family. No player is going to choose a football club over their kid. That far outweighs any idea of us dying for the badge. I get that fans lose their heads with footballers, but don't ever think we aren't trying. Players want to do well, because if they don't they're risking their job. And think about it: 99 per cent of the time playing for the shirt and playing for yourself is the same thing. The better you do for yourself the better you do for the shirt. Even if you want to get away from a club, you're not going to make that happen by having a stinker every week. Who's going to sign you if your team gets relegated and you're a big part of the reason why? The only possible outcome of not trying is that your money goes down with your performance and that affects yourself and those you care for.

Having said that, there are games where players will dig deeper to give that little bit extra. Look at local derbies. You could argue that if players aren't bothered about the badge then the opposition shouldn't make any difference. But derbies do mean something to players, because they're so big for the fans. I've always wanted to play my very best, to do it right, for the supporters. And when it comes to derbies, doing it right matters even more. You want your fans to have the bragging rights, to see their mate at work on Monday and say, 'We got one over you!' Derbies are a must-win. That's when you see the manager really lift a team in the dressing room, hammering into them exactly what the following 90 minutes mean. How they can't leave anything out there. That's where those extra few percentage points of performance come from. That's why the pace of the game is faster, the challenges harder, the needle between players just that little bit more in your face. Out of all the derbies I've played in, Southampton versus Portsmouth would have to be the most passionate. Those two really don't like each other. You can almost taste the venom in the air. West Ham versus Tottenham always has a bit on it, but it's neither side's big derby. For West Ham, that's Millwall. I would absolutely love to have played in that one – although maybe not at their place! – but, with the Hammers predominantly in the Premier League, meetings have been pretty thin on the ground in recent times.

In some ways, you just can't win with the whole badge debate. You can smile and pat the crest on your shirt all you like, but then not everyone wants to see players enjoying themselves. Some fans get frustrated by it. They want you to be serious because, at the end of the day, it's their club and they want it to win everything. Look like you're breezing around having fun and to them it's like, 'You don't care enough about our club!'

The one thing you never want on your shirt is a target on the back: to be that player identified by the fan base as being half-arsed or no good. Every time you appear you get a load of shit from the crowd, as if they can't wait for you to make a mistake so they can turn to their mate and say, 'I told you so!' I'm talking from experience here. I've been that player. At West Ham, no matter what I did, however many goals I scored, every single year there were fans saying, 'Michail isn't good enough. We need better. Blah, blah.' That could very easily affect your confidence. I was able to deal with it because, no matter what anybody else said, I was always confident in my ability. No matter what dressing room I was in, no matter what my age, I would always tell myself, *I'm one of the best players here.* I've always believed that in my soul. I have to, because if I start doubting myself then I'll also start believing that other players are better than me. And that means they deserve a spot in front of me. How can I go out there and play freely if I feel someone else deserves to be out there more than me? I've always believed I'll do a better job than anybody. But when a crowd is on your back it takes a strong mentality to shut out the noise. Professional football is sport's most unforgiving environment. I've played in matches where fans have cheered one of their own players getting subbed off. Do the people doing that ever stop to think how that must feel for the player concerned? Forget football, it's a horrible way to treat someone, full-stop. A player can carry that rejection with them for a long time. Does anyone deserve that just for trying to go about their job?

It doesn't matter who we are or what we do, none of us is perfect. But the minute a footballer steps over the white line, that seems to be forgotten. We should actually be happy players make mistakes, because that's often where moments of excitement come from – a player upends an opponent and gives a free-kick away on the edge of the penalty area, or a defender makes a wayward back pass. Let's imagine a game where every footballer plays to perfection. How boring it would be.

Considering how much grief they get, it's no surprise when a player's elastic snaps. Look at Jarrod Bowen being pulled away from the travelling West Ham fans after losing at Wolves in the early rounds of the Carabao Cup in 2025. The skipper had gone across to applaud the Hammers' following but then reacted angrily to something a supporter shouted and had to be held back from a confrontation by his teammates. Forget the game, that's the moment that gets all the headlines. The media act all shocked that a professional footballer, with all the rewards that position brings, could behave like that. But there's a limit to what anyone can take as a human being. I know Jarrod personally. He gives 100 per cent every single time he steps out on that field. So, if you're in his face telling him he's not trying, maybe giving him a load of abuse, when the truth is he's out there grafting, doing everything he possibly can for the club and the team, and his teammates are doing the same, then his tolerance is going to be pushed to the wire. He'll know immediately he shouldn't have reacted that way, but as captain he has to stand up for his team. He also needs the fans to stick with him and his players. When a team is struggling, that's the exact moment they need supporting. When fans keep getting on players' backs they only succeed in pushing them further into the gutter. If you're constantly hammering somebody who's already down, how can you ever expect them to get better? So, what was Jarrod's reaction really about that night? It was about passion. It was about his love for the game. And it was about his desire to do his best for the club.

Sometimes as a footballer you just can't win. Whatever's happened in the game, even if you've been battered 4–0, you're expected to go over and clap your away following. Chances are if that's happened there'll be quite a few hurling abuse. I've seen it happen so many times. You've gone over to genuinely thank the fans for their support and in return you've got the finger, people telling you to 'F*** off!' There's been times when I've been tempted to do what Jarrod did and give a bit back, but I can't recall ever actually doing it. I've given it back later on social media but never in the ground itself. Even then, though, I've done it in a cheeky way, rather than properly slating anybody.

There is an alternative of course – disappear straight down the tunnel without acknowledging your support. Not a good idea. You're only going to get a load more stick for being disrespectful. It's a classic Catch-22 situation. My option was always, however dire the performance, to go over and take the stick. At the end of the day, whatever the anger being levelled in your direction, those people have taken the time and shelled out the money to come and see you. Without the fans, the game would be nothing. Forget TV, the money, the big names; the fans are the game's lifeblood and always will be. The vast majority will back the team whatever happens. For every fan having a pop, there's always another asking for your shirt.

Of course, most abuse you get in a football ground comes from the opposition fans, not your own. In the din of a Premier League crowd, unless you're taking a throw-in or corner, you're rarely going to hear individual comments. But there are people out there who can do it. I've been at Jamaica internationals played in America, with zero atmosphere in the stadium, bellowing advice from the dugout, and the boys haven't heard a thing. So, whoever's shouting in the middle of 50,000 fans at an English football ground and making themselves heard knows how to project their voice! I honestly don't understand how they manage it. I was screaming my lungs out at a couple of players, trying to get them to exploit a bit of weakness in the other team, and it wasn't until one of them came across for a drink that he even realised I was trying to communicate with him. I actually have a lot of respect for those English fans and their lungs!

Constant stick is why a lot of players like to goad the opposition supporters when they score, standing in front of them with a hand behind the ear, or celebrating right in front of them. I've never done that whole winding-up thing. If anything, when I score I avoid the fans. I want to leave that moment for me. I get why players do it though. Fans always have something to say, so those few seconds after scoring offer a great opportunity to go back at them a bit. Footballers must be some of the most restrained people on Earth, because the amount of shit aimed at them week in, week out is unbelievable. And they always have to take it. Well, nearly always. Remember the footage of Eric Cantona kung-fu kicking that Crystal Palace fan at Selhurst Park? Fans are allowed to say what they want, do what they want, and we just have to suck it up. As human beings, there's only so many times you can claw at us before we bite back. To be told that no matter what happens we can't react is one of the most frustrating things about being a footballer. Look at what Cantona was expected to put up with that night. He's already been sent off and then as he's walking down the side of the pitch this 'fan' follows him, goading him, giving him a load of shit, because he thinks he can, quite literally, do whatever he wants and his 'victim' can't do anything about it. But there's only so much anyone can take, and Cantona, in that moment, had reached his absolute limit.

There's no other working environment where people have to put up with that kind of stuff. No-one's stocking shelves in a supermarket with a bunch of people stood behind them calling them every name under the sun. Even in the sporting world, there's no other arena where fans are so opinionated, so happy to dish out abuse. You don't see it in basketball, rugby, cricket, anywhere. I've never watched an American Football game and seen a spectator throwing shade at anybody. But in my game, it happens all the time. No-one bats an eyelid. It's the most normal thing in the world. And the mad thing is, fan behaviour is not as bad as it was. For years they were fighting in the stands. It's a hundred times better now, but even so it's ridiculous how easily people lose their minds. The only explanation is that these are outwardly normal individuals who turn up once a fortnight to a football match to release all their frustration from their lives. They unzip their real skin at the turnstile and then, once the final whistle blows and they're out of the stadium, they just as easily slip back into it. Normal life resumes, as if the previous 90 minutes of utter insanity never happened.

Well, for some it does. Others just transfer their rage to social media – a whole other level of madness. A BBC investigation in 2025 found that more than 2,000 extremely abusive social media posts, including racist slurs, death and rape threats, were sent about managers and players in the Premier League and Women's Super League in a single weekend. As a player, you come to understand very early on that everybody wants to have their say, and with social media they've found exactly the platform to do so. You could literally have the best game of your life but there'll still be someone reaching for their mobile to say you're the worst player there's ever been and you're robbing a living. There was one guy on X who, no matter how I played, would always call me a donkey. It got to the point where after every game I'd end up scrolling through my feed to see what he said because it was so crazy. In a strange way I kind of came to admire him. His commitment to his cause couldn't be faulted!

While that one guy was laughable, it's not easy to ignore every bit of outside noise that comes your way. Everyone, or so it seems, has got something to say, and living in the public eye amplifies every post, positive or negative. You can see a thousand good comments, and then you hit that single negative one and that's it, everything that came before is forgotten. Everybody else could have been telling me I had a blinder and then there it is: 'Nah, sorry mate, you were shit.' There's been times when I've found myself sitting there staring blankly at a post like this and thinking, *How did you come to that conclusion? I know when I've played shit! And when that happens everyone tells me I've played shit. So how, when everyone says I played well, and I believe I played well, have you come to the decision that I've played shit? How does that make any sense to you?*

The worst insult anybody could throw at me is that I'm lazy. There's never been a minute on the pitch when I haven't given my all. Say I'm lazy and I will be annoyed. I've worked my arse off, not just in the game but in everything that makes me the footballer I'm proud to be. It's personal comments like that which can totally mangle your brain if you let them.

I'll be honest, when I was younger I did sometimes reply to online critics. You shouldn't really do it, but I got away with it because I never said anything where the FA could charge me. I recall one guy sent me a message, it was the usual thing – 'You're shit Antonio! You're an absolute disgrace!' – and I couldn't help zooming in on his picture, a big guy wearing a massive baggy V-necked top. 'Looks like you've been trying to do a bit in the gym,' I told him, 'but obviously it's not working for you.' He wasn't massively pleased with that. There was a bit of back and forth. I kept reeling him in and eventually his response was, 'I hope you get AIDS.' I was delighted. The fact he'd resorted to flinging around horrible garbage like that showed I was the bigger and better man.

'That's 10–0!' I told him. 'I've definitely won.'

There was definite satisfaction in doing that, but in truth a footballer can struggle with the weight of negative comments. I've heard people say how just one critical voice among hundreds of positives can feel as if that person is right there in the room. And I agree. There've been times when I've asked myself, *Why are you letting this one comment affect you?* It's grated at me. *Why are you saying I played shit? I did have a good game! I know I did!* Other times I've had a message saying I've played badly and I've thought, *I already know that – why are you telling me?* Alternatively, I'd reject someone's positivity. 'You had a great game!' *Thanks, but I didn't really.* That's how deeply words can affect players. Some will delete the relevant apps to avoid having that kind of shit in their heads. I'm much better at resisting the urge to look now, but I wouldn't say I've completely stopped doing so. It's human nature to want to see what people are saying about you, and to feel hurt or angry if it's something negative. Unlike when I was younger, I do understand the power, the hold, of social media. Back then if someone complained that it was wearing them down, I'd say 'Just stay off it.' But it's such a massive part of everyday life – you get news on it, you connect on it, you see what family and friends are up to – that telling someone simply to avoid it is way too simplistic. Understandably they feel like social media is an essential part of their lives. What would they do without it?

The upshot is that a lot of players step out on to the field with a whole load of criticism lodged consciously or subconsciously in their heads. That's not great. The game's tough enough as it is. What has helped me down the years is, again, that indestructible self-belief. People can call me a donkey all day, but I know I get the job done. Self-belief really is everything at the top end of football. There will always be people around you with opinions, especially when you're operating in an area as high-profile as the Premier League. The only answer is to trust in yourself and the fact that what you're doing is right. There was never a defender who I thought, *Shit! I'm up against him this week*. I always felt that physically I could handle myself against anybody. Virgil van Dijk was different class: quick, strong, fast, intelligent, always in the right places. The full package. But there's always something you can do to make your life easier. In Virgil's case, my way of countering him was simple – avoid him as much as possible. I'd go up against him if I had to, but generally I'd stay more towards the right-sided centre-half. They'd make it an easier day! Again, it's about finding an answer and trusting in it.

At least attacks on social media exist somewhere in the virtual world. There are players out there who have felt the physical wrath of so-called fans. You only have to look at Jack Grealish getting punched in the face by a pitch invader at the Birmingham City–Aston Villa derby to see how vulnerable footballers are to random attacks by the crowd. In fact, the only surprise is it doesn't happen more often. I've never been set upon myself, but I was at Sheffield Wednesday when our goalkeeper Chris Kirkland was shoved in the face and knocked to the ground by a Leeds United fan at Hillsborough. I remember at the time thinking how lucky that fan was. The day before the game Chris's back was playing up and Stephen Bywater was going to be in goal. Stephen's an absolute monster among men. He knows martial arts, the lot. I'm not scared of many people, but I'm scared of Stephen! Had that Leeds fan tried punching him, he'd have known about it big-time.

Pitch invasions at the end of a game can also be dodgy. When West Ham lost to Eintracht Frankfurt in the Europa League semi-final, a fan ran up to me with his phone on Snapchat. 'Ey, what's up bro? What's wrong bro? What's wrong bro?' Obviously, I was totally pissed off, but I wasn't going to tell him that. Unfortunately, my silence wasn't going to make any difference. This idiot just wasn't going away. He just kept talking and talking – 'How do you feel?' – really pissing me off. In the end, I couldn't take anymore. 'My money's good though,' I told him. I regret saying that now, but it was said in the heat of the moment. Money isn't the be-all and end-all, of course it isn't. The clip then went viral. People were leaving comments. 'Why did you have to say that to him?' Hang on! He was the one who came on the pitch chatting rubbish to me, trying to piss me off. Am I supposed to just take it? No, I'm going to say something to piss him off back. How come it's OK for him to get in my face and not the other way round? If someone does that to me, I'll say what I want to say. People who don't like it are the ones who should stay quiet.

Frankfurt was that classic case of fans swarming on to the pitch at the end of the game. I had to make my way through them to get to the tunnel, but aside from the guy with the phone no-one really troubled me. Even so, those invasions can be unnerving. In recent seasons there's been a few incidents where players have been attacked at the end of EFL play-off games. When you're suddenly plunged into the middle of thousands of fans, potentially not always friendly, you're in a vulnerable position. Thankfully, the only time I've experienced a pitch invasion in England was when I was at Sheffield Wednesday and we beat Wycombe Wanderers on the last day of the season to secure promotion from League One. On that occasion there were 38,000 ecstatic Wednesday fans in the ground. As the game neared its conclusion, my only concern was getting out of the way of the avalanche of supporters set to fill the pitch and get the celebrations underway. Trouble was, I was playing on the right side – and the tunnel was on the left. As the minutes wound down, I asked the ref how long left. 'Thirty seconds,' he replied. That was it. I was off to the left-hand side. There was me and our left-winger Jermaine Johnson stood next to each other playing the same position! Seconds later the whistle went and the place went mental. Even though I was right next to the tunnel, I only just made it out the way in time.

Players can be similarly vulnerable when they're out and about on their own time. I've never actually had a fan of another club give me grief on a night out. Obviously, I'm glad that's the case, but it wouldn't bother me if it did happen. What does it matter? Whatever they say is just an opinion, and one that belongs to someone who isn't important to me. Respond to crap like that and you're giving that person precisely what they're looking for. They know they've got under your skin. Chances are they're also looking for an excuse to escalate the situation. If someone's been drinking, things can get out of hand very quickly.

I do occasionally get people having a little prod. It happened the other day. I was walking down the street in London when a few guys came alongside me. 'You're Michail Antonio aren't you?' one of them asked. He was OK, but one of his friends wanted to be funny. 'Bro, you're shit.' I was like, 'OK, no problem.' He followed me, saying the same thing over and over. 'You're shit, bro.' At one point I went into a shop. I came out and he was still there, saying the same stuff, staring me in the face, clearly trying to get a reaction, to bug me until we'd get into an altercation. I didn't take the bait. He was an embarrassment, both to himself and to his friends, and I wasn't going to let him trouble me. He made a fool of himself, I disappeared and that was that.

Thankfully, the vast majority of approaches from fans are nothing but friendly. I can still remember the buzz of signing my first autograph when I went pro at Reading. When initially I arrived at the Madejski, nobody knew who I was, nobody cared. But as time went on and I started to pop up in the first team, I'd get asked for autographs more and more, especially since the car park was a good 300 yards from the players' entrance. Initially, I just put my normal signature. An older head soon advised me that it wasn't the best idea to go with the same signature as on my bank card, driver's licence, passport, etc. So I changed it, but doing so felt weird. I didn't have a clue what I was going to write, so much so that I had to go home and practise! Of course, no sooner had I perfected my autograph than suddenly everyone had a phone in their hand and it was all about selfies. That constant demand for pictures can irritate a lot of players, but personally I see it as nothing but a compliment. The only time it bugs me is when I'm in a restaurant with my family. I'll never do a selfie in those circumstances. For me, that's just rude. I'm always, 'I'll do it once I finish eating.' A fan might think that's me being up myself, but the way I see it, no chance would I interrupt someone I admired while they were busy with their family. It's just basic manners.

But then again footballers often get made out to be behaving badly when they're doing nothing of the sort. Look at what happens when they turn up at a ground. A lot of boys will step off the team bus with headphones on and go straight into the stadium. Meanwhile, there'll be people trying to get selfies and autographs. It can look selfish, especially if there's kids there, but you have to remember that once players leave the pre-match hotel their whole focus is on playing the game. For a lot of them, music is a big part of getting into the zone. They've got a job to do and they don't want any distractions. It's the same with a lot of jobs in that people need to be absolutely tuned into what they do. It might just be a psychological thing – feeling that they've done everything to maximise performance – but it's become an important part of their routine and so they stick to it like glue.

Not everyone's like that. Some players are chilled and relaxed before a game so don't mind going over to the fans and signing a few things. Personally, I'm a bit of both. I can be nervous before a game to the extent I wouldn't want to interact with anybody, not even the other boys in the changing room. There've been times when I've lain down in my little cubby hole with my hat and my headphones on and the boys have genuinely thought I'm asleep. Actually, I'm just there in my own little world. If I'm not in the team, it's a totally different story. I'll happily interact with fans, go over and have a chat, whatever they want. Some players prefer to get in the zone by having music on in the dressing room. Generally, that'll be house or rap, the sort of music to get everyone really pumping. But it's each to their own. Not everyone wants to be part of that big communal vibe. They'll want to get in the mood their own way and so will stick their headphones on. I'm one of those.

However strained relationships can get with fans, no matter what the chants or abuse, no player would ever wish to repeat the experience of Covid. From playing in cauldrons in front of thousands of noisy and excitable supporters, we were catapulted into soulless and empty stadiums. It was like existing in a vacuum, every last little bit of atmosphere removed, to the extent that the first few Premier League games under lockdown restrictions felt like reserve matches. You could quite literally hear everybody shouting to each other. At West Ham it was something we had to get used to – and quickly. We were in a relegation scrap and couldn't fall into the trap of taking our foot off the gas. Psychologically, that would have been all too easy. The atmosphere in the ground is part of what keeps you fighting and alert. The noise drives you on as an individual and a team. When it's lacking, it's easy to lose a few percentage points of performance. We had to make sure that mentally and physically we were totally switched on.

People will say it shouldn't make a difference if a crowd is there or not, but of course it does. In a reserve game, for instance, you can hear your fellow players. They can help you out. Turn!', 'Man on!', 'Here!' In a packed stadium, those same players might still be shouting, but no way will you hear them, and so you end up playing on instinct a lot more. You make totally different decisions. The other thing to bear in mind is that in an empty stadium you've got the manager in your ear. They know you can hear them and so are going to be on at you all the time. Play in front of a full house, on the other hand, and even if you can still hear the boss screaming and shouting you can easily pretend that you can't! When Covid came, that particular small pleasure was gone.

Of course, you can't beat the atmosphere that fans bring to the game, but I do believe that the quality of the football during Covid was better. Why? Because players could perform without the added pressure that crowds bring, whether that's from their desperation for the team to win or the moans and groans that inevitably come when things aren't going to plan. With no-one in the stands, the only pressure comes from yourself, to perform well, and from your teammates. The flipside is of course the incredible boost the fans deliver when they're backing you, when you hear them singing your name. For a frontman, not having them there is perhaps weirdest of all. The biggest rush on a football field comes from sticking the ball in the net and seeing the crowd go crazy. I scored one of the best goals of my career, a bicycle kick, against Manchester City in October 2020. Normally that would have got a massive reaction. In my head, I was actually waiting for it. And then – SILENCE. There was absolutely nobody there. Typical. I score a worldie against one of the best teams on the planet and the only ones to see it are the players, officials and the coaches. It did happen though. You have to believe me. Go on YouTube and check!

There's something else about lockdown I've considered. It was during that period that I lost my dad. At that time, if people had been shouting stuff at me from the sidelines I might well have reacted. The fact stadiums were empty made it much easier to deal with. Again, it's something I expect most people don't think about when they're giving players a load of crap. While we all try to leave our private lives in the dressing room, there are some things that simply can't be forgotten for 90 minutes.

When you think of it like that, the only surprise is there aren't players confronting fans in the stands every week.

SEVEN
RACISM

I'm a 12-year-old playing the game I love when a kid on the opposition team calls me a monkey. My initial reaction is to try to fight him on the pitch. I don't – I'm not able to get to him. Instead, my team does the right thing and reports it to the FA. The result is me and the other kid attend a hearing.

On arrival, I'm faced with three old white guys. They'll make the decision on what happens next. Before we go into the actual hearing, they tell me, 'We're not going to ask you any questions. We're just going to speak to the adults.' But they don't. In fact, all they do is talk directly at me, questioning me again and again on everything surrounding the incident. It's me under scrutiny. Me who has to explain myself. There's not a lot to say. 'I told you what's happened,' I say to them. 'That's the situation, and this is where we're at.' Meanwhile, the other kid

*just sits there. He doesn't have to answer a single
question. In the end, I leave the room. It's obvious
nothing is going to happen.*

And nothing does.

Looking back now on that FA hearing, I can see how
everything was totally weighted against me. To say I was
upset at the outcome would be an understatement. I'd wanted
to fight the kid but instead had done things the right way and
reported it, thinking he'd be punished, and still it hadn't
worked out for me. The people who were supposed to sort
this stuff out, lay down a marker, make sure it didn't happen
again, had totally failed me – and everyone else in the same
position. I left that building with a whole load of pent-up
frustration and pain. If anything, I just wanted to fight that
kid even more. I learned only one thing from the entire experience. If you say anything about being racially abused, it'll
be completely ignored.

That was 23 years ago. A lot has happened in that time –
just look at all the technology we have in our lives, the electric
cars, the phones, the internet – and yet how much has really
changed when it comes to attitudes to racism? In football, the
punishment for illegal betting is much harsher than it is for
being racist. Same with missing a drugs test. Either of those
and you're banned from playing for months, possibly years.
Say something racist to a fellow player and you're out for a
handful of games. Priorities are wrong. I've seen it happen
time and time again. A few years ago, Huddersfield Town
were fined £50,000 for breaching the Football Association's

rules on shirt sponsorship. At the same time, Millwall were forced to stump up a £10,000 penalty after their fans came out with racist chants in an FA Cup tie. Leeds United, meanwhile, were fined £200,000 for spying on Derby County during a training session.

Remember a while back when my then West Ham teammate Kurt Zouma got in trouble for a video which showed him kicking his cat? I asked at the time whether what he'd done was worse than racism? I wasn't downplaying or condoning his actions. It was a serious question. People were calling for him to be sacked, jailed even. Compare that to the short-term ban facing a player who's been racist. Is it me? Or is it blindingly obvious how low down the pecking order racism is in the minds of those in charge of football? You have to ask why that is, and the obvious answer is the lack of diversity at the top of the organisations which run the game. They've never experienced racism so have no understanding of it. I hope any 12-year-old kid who's recently been racially abused on a football pitch is being treated a lot differently to how I was. But until racist conduct is taken seriously by those who wield the power, I won't be holding my breath.

Racism doesn't stop because you're a footballer. If anything it happens more, because the minute you put on a football strip you're dehumanised in the eyes of some people and that means they don't think twice about calling you anything they want. I'm struck by it every week when I look into the stands and see that instant transformation people make from the normal person they must be during the rest of the week, at home, in their job, or whatever, into someone completely different, red-faced, veins throbbing, shouting and bellowing. Look at those who have been taken to court for hurling racist abuse. The stereotype is of some young thug, but it's not that uncommon for them to be middle-aged businessmen. People who might generally be described as 'respectable'. Their friends are all like, 'He's never normally like that.' So, what makes him behave so badly just because he's walked through a turnstile?

Considering I've played almost 600 games, you might find it surprising that I have never been racially abused by someone in a crowd at a football match. That kind of thing tends to happen more on social media. I've had monkey and banana emojis sent to me. The usual stuff from the sad keyboard warriors. But I've never had anything said to my face. Actually, I should rephrase that. I've never *heard* anything said to my face. In 2022, a Leeds United fan was given an eight-week sentence, suspended for 12 months, banned from attending any football match for four years, and ordered to complete 100 hours of unpaid work after hurling racist abuse at me after I scored a last-minute winner when West Ham played at Elland Road the previous year. The supporter also threatened a fellow Leeds fan who rightly challenged him over his outburst, which I think goes to show that crowds are a lot less tolerant of racist behaviour than they used to be. We saw the same thing happen, fans speaking out, when Bournemouth's Antoine Semenyo was racially abused by a spectator at Anfield in the first Premier League match of the 2025–26 season.

Players too now react as one. Whereas in years past a player would generally have to deal with abuse on their own, these days the entire team will be backing them to the hilt. There's a joint attitude of, *We're not having that*, to the extent we've even seen sides walk off the pitch. Everyone has each other's back. The time of players dealing with this kind of shit as individuals has gone. But if the racists are really to be removed from football, then the actions of fans and players have to be backed up by the authorities. The way to do that is to deduct points and order that games be played behind closed doors. Just as with players walking off the field, that kind of zero-tolerance attitude would make everyone in that ground understand just how abhorrent and unacceptable racist language is. The second someone gets up and shouts something, the consequences are massive.

I was born in 1990 so thankfully missed the worst of this kind of behaviour, and not really being a follower of football I didn't see it on TV either, but I know all the stories, about people throwing bananas on the pitch at John Barnes, and all that stuff. I know also that if a player was racially abused on the pitch, chances are it would get dealt with in the tunnel at the end of the game, because react on the field and they'd get a red card.

The abuse players experienced in stadiums only mirrored what was happening on the streets outside. My dad was part of the Windrush generation. He came to Britain from Jamaica in the 1950s, helping to rebuild the country after the war. He told me about his experience in those early years. How some people turned their backs on him despite him quite literally having come across to help the place they lived in. How, once the country was back on its feet, they were like, 'OK, you guys need to leave now.' Dad told me how he shrugged off that kind of prejudice. It was just part of life and that was the end of it.

It's incredible to think that 70 years on, in the 21st century, we're still having to educate ignorant people that racism is wrong. Because that's what it is – ignorance. People with closed minds who spout off without ever even thinking about what they're saying. But that doesn't mean I'm defeatist about it. In football, I've been a big advocate for Kick It Out, the anti-discrimination campaign supported by the Professional Footballers' Association (PFA), Premier League and FA. In 2020, meanwhile, following the death of George Floyd, the unarmed African American man killed during an arrest in Minneapolis by a white police officer, players started taking the knee. I've heard people say they don't know whether this kind of positive action really works, but I certainly felt, in its early days at least, it was an especially powerful way of illustrating the ongoing fight against racism in society. These days the gesture happens less often, as part of October's No Room For Racism fixtures, coinciding with Black History Month. I'm happy with that because if it had carried on at every game it would have lost its impact. If it happens more occasionally then it becomes a talking point again. It retains its power.

I know there's adults who are stuck in their ways when it comes to racism and will never be swayed by a bunch of footballers going down on one knee, but for me it isn't about them, it's about the kids. Think about it. The first time a child sees the players of the club they support taking the knee, they're going to want to know what's going on. At that point they'll be told it's about racism. There's no other way to answer that question. Even if the adult they're with is themselves racist, they've still got to explain. I like that – even racists are inadvertently helping and supporting the cause. Taking the knee isn't about trying to change the views of the older generations, it's about educating the people coming through life after them.

It was having that eye on the future that meant I was happy to back the Premier League's No Room For Racism initiative. I went into a school in Dagenham to encourage children to appreciate the benefits of diversity and resilience, and to face up to prejudice. 'Racism shouldn't exist,' I told them, 'but it does, and we have to try both to oppose it and prevent it.' I wanted them to know that, wherever they might encounter racism, pathways exist to report it and make sure it doesn't happen again. Footballers are actually great role models when it comes to the positivity that diversity brings. If there's any better illustration than a Premier League dressing room of people from all over the world getting along then I don't know what it is. In my last season at West Ham, we had players from France, Poland, Czech Republic, Greece, Italy, Spain, Brazil, Ghana, Mexico, Argentina, the Netherlands, Germany, Ireland, Ivory Coast and Morocco. All of us pulling in the same direction to achieve the same goal. More than that, becoming a second family to one another.

But as much as we can try to change the narrative as footballers, it's vital that others do their bit too. Raheem Sterling was right to highlight the different way that players are treated by the media – a classic case being the comparison he made between newspaper headlines about his then Manchester City teammates Tosin Adarabioyo and Phil Foden buying houses. One stated that Foden, aged 18, had bought 'a £2 million home for his mum'. The other that Adarabioyo, 21, had bought a £2.25 million property 'despite having never started a Premier League match'. Foden's is portrayed as a generous act of kindness, Adarabioyo's as something undeserved. I loved it when Raheem highlighted those headlines, because it's so easy for this undercurrent of unequal treatment to go unnoticed. Like so much else, it's based on ignorance, but no longer are players sitting back and letting people get away with it. Again and again, we see both outdated opinions and downright abuse being challenged. There is unity now among the vast majority of players and supporters that enough is enough, a strength of feeling which means it is now the racist in the stand who feels the odd one out, who hopefully will think twice about their behaviour, and, if they're unwilling to change, never return to the football environment.

It's a stance that has to be backed up by those who run the game. That 12-year-old kid can't ever be let down again.

EIGHT
PLAYERS

'Pheeep!'

He's at it again.

*We're playing Manchester City. Every time Nicolás
Otamendi wants the ball off a teammate he makes a
whistling sound, like he's blowing air through his
teeth.*

*It pisses me off. That 'Pheeep!' goes straight
through me. Like someone scraping their nails down
a blackboard. I'd love to know if Otamendi does it
on purpose. I reckon he does. He must know it will
irritate people. Why else would he do it all the time?*

*'Pheeep!' – there it is again. I try to calm myself,
but it's not easy. I really want to kick the shit out of
him. I can't stand that noise in my head. I mutter
under my breath, 'For f***'s sake. Use your voice!'*

*Players – some you get on with. Some you'd like to
put in Row Z.*

In football there's always someone trying to get on your wick. Surprising then that the only player I've ever properly lost my rag with is the Chelsea right-back Reece James. He kept grabbing hold of my shirt, holding on to me: half-footballer, half-limpet. It was like playing against a tube of superglue. I was raging. 'What are you doing? Get the f*** off me! Who do you think you're holding bro?' It's the only time I've lost my head on a football field to the point where I wanted to fight somebody. 'OK, how about we don't sort this out here? How about we do it in the tunnel?'

Sorry fight-fans, but the showdown never actually happened. Eventually, perhaps fearing for his own safety, Reece gave me an explanation for his actions. 'Look,' he told me, 'I have to give you some grief. I don't want anyone watching to think I'm scared of you!'

OK, right, now I understood. The moment passed and by the end of the game we were cool again. Good job, really. Crazy thing is, me and Reece had the same agent. But in the heat of professional football, being in the same team off the pitch was irrelevant. Emotions don't operate like that.

Football's such a high-pressure environment that there's bound to be conflict, but while the footage of Roy Keane straining on the leash to get at Patrick Vieira in the Highbury tunnel is legendary, big bust-ups aren't that common. I've certainly never seen it kick off as the teams line up to go out before the game. If anything, that's a time when you're keeping yourself to yourself, just getting your head right for what's about to come. The last thing you need is a face-off with a member of the opposition. On the pitch is where the aggression comes in. But even then, players know they need to rein it in. You're hardly going to be in the manager's good books if you reduce his side to ten men. That's why the tunnel is often a bit tastier at half or full-time. 'Right, we'll have to take it inside, because you ain't being bad with me!'

In some ways being a footballer is no different to any other working environment. Some people you get on with, some you don't. There are teammates who dislike each other so much they won't speak to each other, except for on the pitch itself. At that point, you have to communicate for the good of the side. Otherwise, nothing. But what tends to happen more often is a momentary bust-up on the training ground, something which can blow up out of nowhere. Even players who are pretty good mates can lose it with one another. A kick in the wrong place and you can soon find yourself in trouble. You're talking about very competitive people. It's inevitable they'll occasionally lose their heads.

I had a front-row seat for one of the best training-ground fights I ever saw – because I was in it. Mark Noble absolutely clattered me in a tackle, something which rarely goes down well among players desperate to avoid injury and maintain their place in the team. I was no different. I was spewing, to the extent that when I dragged myself off the floor, I grabbed hold of Nobes and rubbed his face in the dirt. He wasn't massively pleased with my reaction, and, with Nobes not exactly being a character who likes to back down, matters might have got properly out of hand had a few of the other boys not rushed in to intervene in the melee. These fights don't last long. It's not like the playground where everyone gathers round while a couple of lads scrap for five minutes. The other players will be straight in there to break it up. It's why you never see these things on pay-per-view.

Unfortunately, if I wasn't actually in the fight, it always seemed like I missed it. Which is disappointing – you want to be there those days! But one I do remember at West Ham involved our midfielder Flynn Downes. Flynn could be a fiery boy, and in this case ignited a belter of a scrap with Jarrod Bowen. In a training drill, Flynn stepped on Jarrod's ankle a couple of times. The forward was having none of it and squared up to him. 'What the f*** do you think you're doing?' Flynn came straight back. 'Shut the f*** up!' 'What? Who do you think you're talking to?' 'Come on, then, let's f***ing go!' 'OK, let's f***ing go!' And that was it – Flynn punched Jarrod in the face. I don't think anyone could quite believe what had happened. Even Jarrod was stood there in shock. 'He f***ing hit me!' Which shows actually how rare it is for those training-ground spats to get properly out of hand.

Thankfully, players mostly take their frustrations out on the opposition, not their own. Reading's Cameroonian defender André Bikey was something else though. Forever getting into scuffles, be it on the pitch or at the training ground, Bikey had all the ingredients of a bloke you wouldn't want to get on the wrong side of: short-tempered, massive, could really handle himself. When I first started playing, I noticed that every game, after the very first aerial challenge with André, the opposition striker would go down holding the back of his head. After four or five incidents of this happening, I felt I needed to ask what was going on.

'André, how come you always manage to miss the ball and head the striker instead?'

André was very matter of fact. 'I do it on purpose,' he replied. 'Very first header, I don't go for the ball, I butt the back of their head.'

'Yes, but why?'

'Because after that they don't want to head it again.' Like it or not, you can't fault the guy's logic.

Reading seemed to attract these kinds of characters. Centre-back Alex Pearce was another. He used to kick people for fun, again in training and in the games themselves, putting in big, big, challenges of a kind that would make anyone else on the pitch wince. Teammates and opposition players alike were always losing their heads with him. But Alex wasn't a fighter. He'd be like, 'Calm down! We're playing football! Shut up!' While everyone else was standing there in amazement (or rubbing their bruises), he'd grab the ball and carry on like nothing had happened.

Fair to say that some players have thicker skin than others. When West Ham played Manchester United at Old Trafford in 2020, I was accused of mocking Paul Pogba. It was one of the funniest things I've ever seen on a football pitch. Declan Rice took a long-range free-kick which arrowed like a missile straight towards Pogba's head as he stood in the penalty box. A player has two options in that situation. Get the hell out of the way. Or let it hit him. Pogba, however, instinctively raised his hands to defend himself, before falling dramatically to the ground grabbing his face, clearly hoping the ref would think the ball had missed his hands and ploughed into his kisser. The ref was having none of it and awarded the penalty, which I scored to put us 1–0 up on the stroke of half-time. When we went back out for the second half, I happened to be stood near United midfielder Bruno Fernandes and was just mimicking Pogba's hands-up action when the Sky cameras zoomed in on me. I didn't realise at the time but Paul was stood right behind me. Everyone watching at home was treated to the sight of the French World Cup winner giving me absolute daggers. To be fair, by the time the match ended, all was forgotten, and Paul was totally fine with me as we walked back to the tunnel.

Richarlison was a little different. The Brazil and Tottenham Hotspur number nine had a habit of pulling his shirt off after scoring, and after he did it again in a defeat at Liverpool in 2023, I thought it was worth a mention to Callum Wilson, my co-host on BBC's *The Footballer's Football Podcast*. I found it especially amusing that on one occasion, at Fulham, Richarlison had whipped off his top, receiving the mandatory booking along the way, only for the goal to be ruled out by VAR. When a clip of our chat found its way on to TikTok, Richarlison appeared to have a massive sense of humour failure. 'How many goals do both have in the World Cup?' his own account replied, in a dig at me and Callum. Spurs interim manager Ryan Mason also got involved, defending his striker and saying he didn't 'really like that type of thing'. I thought his words were ridiculous. We were all grown men. What Richarlison had done was idiotic in my eyes and I was allowed to say so.

At West Ham we had our own Brazilian, attacking midfielder Lucas Paquetá. I thought I'd have a word with him about Richarlison. 'What's wrong with your boy?' I asked. 'It's just a bit of banter. Why's he taking it to heart?'

All Lucas could really say by way of explanation was that Richarlison is 'made that way'. Lucas had explained to Richarlison that I was just messing around but it had made no difference. As far as Lucas's international teammate was concerned, he was unhappy with me and most definitely wouldn't be going out of his way to be pally when we played against each other in the future. Sadly, that never happened. Shame, because it meant there was never that 'Will he? Won't he?' moment with the pre-match handshake. I'd definitely have offered Richarlison my hand. If he'd refused, bingo! I'd have known at that moment I owned him and was living rent free in his head.

Most players are absolutely fine with a bit of banter – you can imagine in the rough and tumble of the dressing room there's plenty of it – so I don't really get quite why Richarlison took such offence. But he did, and that's fine. It's not like it was a problem to me. And anyway, what he did *was* crazy. If you're going to take your top off, at least wait until you know you've scored a goal! But obviously that's Richarlison's personality and so he'll carry on flashing his upper half at anyone who wants to see it – and all those who don't.

There'll always be players who can't deal with banter, by which I mean friendly joking around, nothing worse. If they happen to be in your own dressing room, it's especially hilarious. The more they lose their heads, the more it makes you want to wind them up. The trick is to find the sweet spot – the point just before things get violent. 'I'm so in your head, man. I'm so living in there rent free!' That's why boys miss the changing room so much in retirement. It's just *so* funny.

There is, however, a lesser known, or perhaps lesser spoken about, truth regarding relationships between players. Beneath the surface of dressing room culture, real and lasting close friendships are hard to come by. In football, it's not as easy as you might think to form that kind of companionship. The very nature of the game means players are coming and going all the time. No sooner have you become mates with someone than they're out the door. It can be the case where you're close to another player while they're at the club and then the minute they leave you never speak to them again.

There's a huge churn in football that you just don't get in a lot of 'normal' jobs which means, like most players, I've gone through my career making acquaintances rather than friends. I've got a handful of players who I'd properly describe as friends, the likes of Ashley Fletcher, Darren Randolph, Angelo Ogbonna, Shaun Cummings, Bobby Reid and Joel Latibeaudiere. A few of those boys have Jamaican heritage, which has always been a big point of connection for me. It's not that I seek people out who have a similar background to me, I just feel naturally drawn to them. It's the same when I go away with Jamaica. Again, the bond I have with those lads compared to players at the clubs I've played for is totally different. Being with them feels so relaxed, so chill. We genuinely enjoy and want to spend time together, whereas at football clubs, interactions tend to be more functional. You train, you go home, you play. On repeat. With

Jamaica, we're spending a lot of quality time with one another. We're in the hotel together. We're going to the beach together. Constantly mixing. At one point, me, Bobby and Joel missed each other so much when we were back home that we started going to boxing matches together. So many relationships in football don't have any depth, so when you do find meaningful friendship it's pretty special, and something you want to hang on to.

Of course, a dressing room full of strangers is no good to anyone, and so senior players will do their best to engender team spirit in any way they can. When I started out, that would mean big boozy nights out. Wherever I went early in my career there was always a big drinking culture. In those dressing rooms there'd be older players who'd been around when, by all accounts, the most respected player was the biggest drinker, the biggest shagger. I'd heard all the stuff about how in the 1980s and 1990s players would wear binbags in training to sweat out the booze from the night before. That kind of old-school approach to drinking was just coming to an end when I got started, and now it's totally gone. Today the most respected player is the one who's done the most at the club. It's on the pitch, not off it, that matters. Achievement is what brings you respect.

Oddly, it wasn't a senior pro who most led me astray on the drinking front. It was Jacob Mellis, a player a year younger than myself, who I got friendly with at Southampton. Jacob's best known for being sacked by Chelsea after setting off a smoke grenade at the club's Cobham training ground, sparking a full-scale evacuation. Before that incident, he was out on loan at the Saints. I wasn't a big drinker. Two Jack Daniel's and Cokes and that was me done. But a night out with Jacob was different. He had a rule – two drinks in your hand at all times. There were occasions when a few of us would be out drinking and the table would be packed with Jägermeisters. We'd be going at it, shot after shot. So many nights, I'd find myself slumped over a toilet bowl throwing up. In later life, Jacob would admit to having issues with alcohol, and that makes sense. A talented boy, he should have achieved much more than he did, but even in the short time I knew him at Southampton I could see his life was pretty chaotic. I went to his house once and it was clear from the lack of basic essentials that he wasn't looking after himself properly.

I'm not going to lie, though, I really enjoyed that year. I had a lot of fun. It wasn't just Jacob. I'd go out with a few players and have a few more drinks than I possibly should have. Wednesday was a day off, which meant generally there'd be a big midweek piss-up on the Tuesday night. After the match on a Saturday, meanwhile, players might carry on drinking through Sunday and on into early Monday. I'll be honest, there were times when I'd turn up to training still drunk from the night before. I couldn't even see the ball let alone do anything constructive with it. The worst was if we were doing crossing and heading drills. The last thing I wanted was that ball thudding into my skull. It felt like my whole brain was exploding. There's no way you could do that now. Most managers would come down on such behaviour like a ton of bricks, but at Southampton Alan Pardew was much more of a hands-off manager than most. As long as I did what he asked on matchdays, he didn't really care what I got up to in-between. 'If you ain't ready for Saturday and get dropped, then that's your fault,' he'd tell me. 'Do what you want during the week, but if you perform on the weekend, then I'll have nothing to say to you. On the other hand, if you don't play well you're going to lose your spot, and that's going to affect your career more than it's going to affect mine.'

The problem came when I went back to Reading and thought I could carry on with the same malarkey. Wrong! I was caught out again and again. Personal responsibility was a lesson I needed to learn. At one point I was fined two weeks' wages. Worse, for two months I was sat on the bench because the manager, Brian McDermott, wouldn't play me. That brought me back down to earth with a bump. It made me realise that the drinking, the late nights, weren't something I could do as a professional footballer. And that was entirely right. Athleticism is so big in the game now. It's all about nutrition and trying to get more out of the body for longer. Alcohol, meanwhile, is a poison. It might give you a lift in the short-term but it certainly doesn't do anything for your body.

Football's more competitive than it's ever been. Players need to look after themselves if they're going to play for as long as they want to. Even across my own career, times have changed. Only in the last decade has healthy living really kicked in as an absolute requirement. There was no real advice on nutrition when I started out. Food within the football clubs I played for was always nutritious. Chefs would always try to keep everything high-protein, only the best fuel. But as soon as I got home, it was all down to me. Starting out at Reading, I'd be calling at McDonald's pretty much every day on my way home from training. I was a sweet monster too, with a cupboard absolutely packed with Haribo and all sorts. I was the absolute worst when it came to nutrition. It wasn't until I reached 27 or 28 that I started eating right. The science on sugar intake made me sit up and take notice. Research shows a connection between consumption and muscle inflammation, which itself can lead to injury. I never had muscle injuries until I got to the Premier League, and then I had three on the bounce. I kept pulling my hamstrings. Something needed to change. Anything I could do to stop that happening, I'd do it. I quit drinking for a while and then cut the sweets down massively. Both acts meant less sugar in my system. That kind of self-control is an absolute requirement. Clubs can't keep an eye on you 24 hours a day. They can weigh you, test your hydration levels, measure your body fat, but the discipline to keep your body ticking over at its best is ultimately down to the individual. I'll own up to still liking a biscuit though!

This adherence to a more healthy regime means that, whereas before, the boys would be out drinking together once or twice a month, big team-bonding nights barely happen anymore. That's fine as far as it goes, but, while some people might frown at that sort of behaviour, seeing it as old-school and unprofessional, there is an argument that those boozy teams were often the ones that achieved the most. The bonding element of drinking is underestimated. I often think you don't really know someone until you've got drunk with them, and in football, where teammates come and go with alarming regularity, it can be a good shortcut to forming links and friendships.

Make no mistake, walking into a football club for the first time isn't for the faint-hearted. It's definitely nerve-wracking, and so you might think there'd be a bit of a welcoming committee, a few people to make you feel comfortable. At the very least you'd maybe expect the captain to be on hand to introduce you to your new teammates. But what happens is you pretty much just turn up at the training ground, shake a few hands, and go out and start doing what you're told to do. For me, that was the same at West Ham as when I started out at Reading. The difference was that at Reading, with it being my first club, I didn't know how to handle it. As a result, I'd sit in the canteen at the training ground with my headphones on and eat on my own. Eventually, Michael Duberry came over and ripped them from my ears. 'Do you not want to know the players you work with?'

'Yeah,' I replied. 'Of course.'

'Then why are you being so anti-social?'

I thought about it. 'But you guys have been here for years. Isn't it your job to be social to me?'

At that point he put me under his wing and introduced me to everybody. I felt much more integrated into the team, but it was a few weeks later, when I really let my hair down at the Christmas do, that the rest of the boys got to see the real me. That was the moment I made real bonds, real friends. It remains one of the funniest Christmas dos I've ever been on. Despite the quantities consumed, I remember it like it was yesterday. We piled into a minibus and went to Bournemouth. It was fancy dress, and our Irish striker Noel Hunt came as a bush, constantly leaping into undergrowth, disappearing and jumping out on people. He was having a great time with this little trick, until he jumped into one particular hedge and landed in a load of dog shit. I can't actually remember my own outfit, possibly because the whole day we were playing drinking games. The maddest was one where someone shouts 'Grenade!' and everyone has to hit the deck. The last to do so has to neck a shot. It didn't matter where you were, what you were doing, if you heard 'Grenade!' down you went. At the same time, if someone shouted, 'Shark attack!' you had to get off the ground at the first opportunity. I was single at the time, enjoying myself talking to a few girls, and the next thing they knew I was either hurling myself to the floor or clambering up on a table. I still look back on that do as one of the most hilarious ever times.

The more moves you make in your career, the more you understand the need to make quick connections to help yourself settle. The result is that it doesn't take long before you gravitate towards certain characters who you feel you'll get along with. In my case, the more comfortable I get with those people, the louder and more boisterous I become, always trying to have that bit of banter. Even as a young player I was pretty lively in the dressing room. I've always had that type of personality. But at the same time, I've never forgotten that feeling when I arrived at Reading, being a bit shy and reserved, and needing someone or something to help me emerge from my shell.

After leaving West Ham in the summer of 2025, it was me who was faced with that challenge of again getting to know a new bunch of people. Training with different teams, I was back to working everyone out a little bit, seeing how they reacted to the different personalities around them, observing the team dynamic. I wondered if it might prove tricky after ten years without a move, but actually it was great to be among different sets of staff and players. Reading the room has always been a big part of me integrating into new environments. When retirement comes it's a skill I hope to put to good use in whatever world I find myself in.

As I progressed in my career, it was me organising gettogethers, knowing how useful they are in terms of allowing newcomers' personalities to come out. I'm in my element on a night out so it was pretty much inevitable that this would happen. I like to play games and always want everybody to have a nice time. I also have friends who own nightclubs, which means players can enjoy themselves in privacy, without cameras being around. That might sound a bit over the top but the press like nothing more than a few pictures of footballers 'misbehaving', although what constitutes misbehaviour as a footballer is generally no different from the kind of stuff that any group of young blokes might get up to after a couple of drinks. Certain elements of the media are especially on the hunt for this kind of stuff if a team is struggling. One time at West Ham, when we were having a stinker in the league, our skipper Mark Noble sorted for us all to go to a restaurant.

What's happening there is a team coming together to relax away from the pressure of performing in the Premier League and strengthening the bonds that will help to get us out of trouble. But you can guess how some journalists portrayed it. Next day, the papers were full of pictures of us laughing and drinking. The narrative was all 'Look at this lot! This is how much they care about West Ham and the supporters.' I expect the restaurant, looking for a bit of free publicity, had tipped them off. If I was organising a night out, at somewhere belonging to a trusted friend, no way was that going to happen.

There's a common misconception that a team on its uppers will find new resolve by drinking cold tea while spending several hours being brutalised on an army assault course. But when you're going through a bad patch, sometimes having a good time makes it better. After that notorious home game against Burnley in 2018 that we lost 3–0, nearly sparking a riot, we were supposed to be flying to Miami for a few days to switch off and regroup. David Moyes had asked for the getaway, a vital mental and physical refresh, and the club had agreed. Sat there despondently in the changing room, we were all thinking, *No way will we still be going after that. The owner's just been pelted with missiles because we lost again, and now he's expected to pay for us to clear off to an American sunspot for a few days?* And then, as we stared at the floor lost in misery and despair, we heard Dave's voice. 'Go on! Get your bags! Just f***ing go!' *Well, if you insist gaffer!* And that was it. Off we went to Miami. Yes, we trained every day, but I, and plenty of the other lads, got steaming every day as well.

Of course, at some point this mini-break in paradise would have to come to an end. Landing on the tarmac, our attention turned to the next game, another we were expected to – and had to – win, Southampton at home. Collecting our bags off the carousel, every player was thinking the same thing. *Oh shit!* The Saints were right there in the mire alongside us. Lose again and who knew what might happen. There were nerves before that game, as there should have been, because nerves focus performance. But after our little freshen-up across the Atlantic we rolled the visitors over 3–0 and went on to finish the season comfortably out of relegation trouble. Sometimes you do just need to have a blowout to get rid of the negativity. It's either that or go home and stare at the wall. I know which one I prefer. From that moment on, any time we were going through a rough patch I was like, 'We're going for a night out!' or 'We're going for dinner!' Anything to build that grittiness, that spirit, between us.

The same goes for fines. While they exist for a reason, to maintain standards and discipline, there's also a fun element to the tradition. At West Ham I was the man in charge, implementing fines ranging from £250 for being late for training to five grand for missing a team dinner. Those fines would then be tallied at the end of the week, at which point offending players would have the option of spinning 'the wheel', a game of complete chance, like the TV show *Wheel of Fortune*, where they could land on 'safe' segments wiping their slate clean, or others doubling or trebling the penalty, even handing it straight to another player. One occasion when Emerson, our Brazilian left-back, chose to spin particularly sticks in mind. 'Emmy' owed £700, I forget what for. Good news was, he landed on a segment which meant the player seated to the left of him in the dressing room had to pay the fine. Scottish midfielder Andy Irving wasn't massively pleased at this turn of events and so spun the wheel himself. The fine went to the player on his right – so straight back to Emmy. Who spun again and, unbelievably, fired it straight back to Andy. You can imagine what this was like – all the boys watching on, laughing and cheering. Andy was having none of it. He spun again, and this time the fine went to the player on his left, Tomáš Souček. Up got Tomáš, spun the wheel. Slowly, it came to a halt – 'TREBLE!' We were absolutely wetting ourselves.

At the end of the day, football is a selfish sport. You look after yourself by doing everything you can to the best of your ability. Do that and you're reaping the benefits for yourself and your family. But at the same time, you can't succeed without your teammates. It has to be 11 acting as one. That's why, the majority of the time at least, players will put their own interests on the backburner to make the right decision for the team. They won't take that strike on goal if there's a teammate in a better position. They'll drain energy reserves tracking back to defensive positions. They'll run the ball into the corner in the 90th minute rather than test the goalkeeper and risk giving away possession. Players know that, ultimately, why they're on the pitch is not to act for themselves but to get the win for the team. By doing that they're effectively killing two birds with one stone. From a purely financial point of view, the more they help the team succeed, the higher their profile becomes and the more they can argue for a better contract. Similarly, the more they collect those win bonuses. At the same time, of course, they can enjoy the day-to-day of being in and around a successful group. Winning changes everything. Go in on a Monday morning and everyone's got a smile on their face. You can't put a price on a positive atmosphere. It's worth everything and hopefully will lead to the kind of big blowouts that nobody can criticise you for! After the victory parade through east London to celebrate our Europa Conference League win, we piled on to a private jet to go to Pablo Fornals' wedding in Spain. Even for a Premier League footballer, that's a pretty mad 48 hours.

Of course, there are times, especially in the heat of the battle, when a trip to Miami – or a high-class wedding in the Med – isn't quite what's needed to boost performance. A 15-minute window at half-time doesn't really allow for such luxuries. It's then that, as well as the manager, you might have one of your fellow pros in your face. As West Ham captain, Mark Noble could certainly do a bit of shouting. He'd proper dig players out. 'You need to be f***ing better!' He'd use the same trick as Moyes, targeting one of the bigger personalities to try to get everybody lifted.

Because of the rewards that come from being a successful footballer, that side of the game as a harsh results-orientated working environment isn't always appreciated. Football is unforgiving, which means when the opportunity comes to lighten the mood you need to take it. Having to train on Christmas Day, for instance, is a bind. In an ideal world, everyone would rather be at home with their family. I'd try to liven things up a little by wearing a different Christmas outfit every year, having a laugh and a mess about with the other boys before putting a picture up on my social media. In 2019, I decided to go into Christmas Day training as Olaf from *Frozen*. That entailed a full snowman bodysuit plus a carrot nose held on with elastic. Normally, I'd change out of this kind of clobber before getting back in my car, but this year I kept it on for a bit of fun while I was visiting family in my Lamborghini Huracan. I'd been to my sister's and was on my way to my mum's when I skidded on ice on a tight bend and lost control. Next thing I knew I was halfway through someone's garden wall and the car was filling with what I thought was smoke – actually it was just a bit of gas from the airbags going off. Either way, I panicked and jumped out as quick as I could. Normally, while I'm sure it would get a bit of attention from people in the immediate vicinity, an event like this would go by pretty much unnoticed by the wider world. But when it's a well-known Premier League footballer, in a Lamborghini Huracan, wearing a snowman suit, it tends to cause a bit of a stir. Which meant everyone in a 100-yard radius whipping out their mobile phones to take pictures, some of which were soon appearing on social media and the big newspaper sites.

You can guess the reaction next time I saw the West Ham boys. 'Hang on, you were still in the snowman costume when you got out the car? You didn't think to take it off?' I was like, 'Look, in the moment you don't think about that kind of stuff. You're not sat there with smoke all around you thinking, "Hang on, let me take my snowman costume off!"' The fans were similarly merciless. When we played at Crystal

Palace the next day they were singing, '*He parks where he likes! He parks where he likes! Michail Antonio, he parks where he likes!*' It's a great chant, but not particularly helpful when you're trying to renew your car insurance. When it came to choosing my next car, the price of cover went through the roof. Companies were trying to charge me £10,000 for an Audi A3, and twice as much for a Mercedes G63. In the end, I paid the twenty grand. I was getting double the car so I might as well pay double the price. At least I could fit my kids in there! Obviously, because I was subsequently involved in another supercar crash, people are like, 'He's a reckless driver.' But I wouldn't say that's true. One accident was down to a patch of ice. The other? Well, I've no idea.

I should say that just because there's noisy players in a dressing room (like me) doesn't mean there isn't room for those who are more introverted. A lot of the time, team nights out will take place over dinner at a restaurant. That gives everyone the opportunity to be together and then the more outgoing players who want to carry on the night can do so. So long as everyone's at the dinner that's all that matters. A few years ago, there would have been that peer pressure for everyone to carry on, but these days no way is anyone going to tell a player they have to be out until the early hours. It's all down to the individual. However, if a player misses a team night, they will get a fine. It's important and there's an expectation that every player be there.

I genuinely believe that, in the modern professional dressing room, everyone should be able to be who they are. No matter what their religion or sexual orientation they should be accepted. Statistically, there must be gay footballers in the game, although, in all honesty, I've never come across anybody – at least anybody that I'm aware of. Which makes me think that, while attitudes have changed, it's still incredibly difficult for a player to come out, and that's to teammates as well as fans. Make no mistake, a professional football changing room is a boisterous place. It's very manly in there. Boys are walking around naked. A lot of the chat is pretty close to the knuckle. I don't doubt football club environments are better than they were. Coming out would be more accepted now than it was when I was first coming through in the game 18 years ago. Boys are much more comfortable now, and understanding, because sexual orientation is so much more spoken about. But I still feel coming out would be an incredibly big step for a player to make. Even if fears about the reaction of teammates proved unfounded, what about the reaction of the crowd? Fans will do anything they can to get under a player's skin. I know for a fact there will always be people shouting stuff at me about my crash. That might be anything from taking the piss out of my driving to telling me they wish I was dead. So, when a gay player steps out on to the pitch, they can 100 per cent expect to get homophobic slurs. Will they want to condemn themselves to that degree of hostility? There's enough pressure as a footballer without heaping on a whole load of added scrutiny.

Then there's the cultural considerations. There's a lot more Muslim players than there used to be. What would their reaction be to a gay player in the dressing room? I'm not saying all Muslims are culturally opposed to gay people, but it's another consideration to add to the question of acceptance. How would it affect the dynamic of the team?

My personal view is that none of us should have to hide who we are. That can really mess with our minds. We should all be free to be who we want. And, as a footballer, how can you possibly express yourself on the field when your mind's not free off it? I don't know how anyone could keep something so massive in their head and keep playing.

I really do hope that if any gay footballers are reading this, they will give being open a try. Look at my own journey. In relation to my mental health, I feel like I myself have come out. Even just a few years ago, who could imagine a Premier League footballer reflecting on their struggle with mental health, talking openly about therapy and elements of their life they've found incredibly hard. When I was younger, I couldn't ever imagine doing that kind of thing. I would have pushed all my deepest emotions down and just carried on as if everything was all right. Even during my hardest times I'd go into training smiling, not able to show what I was really feeling. Now I have a different relationship with emotions. I realise they're OK. More than that, they're the key to dealing with life and everything it throws up along the way.

It's important that footballers are seen as normal people, just like everyone else. Sadly, all too often that's not the case. I'm not looking for sympathy here – I earn more money in a week by kicking a ball than most other people do in a year working in all kinds of challenging and difficult jobs. All I'm saying is that, for a lot of people, the money we earn means that our emotional side isn't allowed to exist. It's as if money in the bank outweighs any personal problem we could possibly have. That's not realistic. Money changes a lot of things – no player will ever complain about earning too much of it – but basic human emotions aren't among them. It's a side of the footballing life that's misunderstood. I'm happy to be open about the effect of money on this footballer's life. Hopefully, along the way, I'll put a few myths to bed. I'll also be honest about everything. The ups. The downs. And the dark avenues where it can lead.

NINE
MONEY

I'm a first-year pro at Reading, staying in digs. There's another young player, himself not on much money, who each morning takes me into training. He's a bit of a gambler, and nearly every day on the way back he stops at a bookies to go on the slot machines. You can get through two or three hundred quid in those places quite quickly and, as I suspect will be the case, he loses more than he wins. The first week I just watch, but after a while I decide to have a try. Nothing crazy. I'm a beginner, so no more than 20 quid. I suppose you could call it beginner's luck but the first few days I win about £200. My lift, meanwhile, is £800 down, and he's not happy.

'You need to give me some of that,' he says.
'What? Why?'
'I'm the reason you won. I brought you here.'
'Yeah, you chose to bring me here! I never asked.'

It's an early sign of how gambling can get a grip of people, how it can change them.
And not in a good way.

I've never really been a gambler, because I don't like losing money – the one thing that gambling absolutely guarantees. I might have won a few quid those first few goes on the slots, but I wasn't drawn in by it. The only time I nearly got sucked in was when I began regularly to find myself on the long coach trips that professional footballers so often have to take. At Southampton, especially, poker was a big distraction on the road to distant away games. I'd played a bit on the bus at Reading, but the stakes there were relatively small. Limits were set. You could only lose a certain amount – 20 quid, 50 perhaps – per hand. At Southampton, though, limits went out the window. At any point you could triple the stake, which meant things could very quickly get out of hand. The situation wasn't helped by the fact the money didn't seem real. It wasn't physically there on the table: bets were just written down in a book. The temptation then was always to push on, to grab the big prize.

On one particular journey, I found myself with a straight flush, king high. I ended up going head-to-head with a teammate. The only thing that could beat me was an ace. I was tripling, tripling, tripling. He was doing the same. *I have a king-high straight flush*, I was thinking, *no way can he have a straight flush with an ace.* We were going back and forth, back and forth, until the pot got to £3,500. I'm on £500 a week at this point. I'm gambling way more than my monthly wage. And it's that scary thought breaking through into my head that finally brings my madness to a halt. *I'm not going any higher. This is it. I'm on a massive winner. I won't be greedy and go again. I'll take what I've got.* Cool as anything I flipped over my cards. *OK! Give me the money!* No prizes for guessing what happened next – my teammate flipped over an ace. *Shit! SHIT!* In that moment all I could think was, *I'm fucked! That's my month's money, and more, literally gone in one game.* That was 100 per cent a lesson learned. In fact, I was lucky. Triple again and I'd have been looking at the best part of 10 grand. From then on, while I still played, I never let it get to the stage where I was betting big money. Even if I had good cards and knew I could win, I'd only triple once and then fold. But I know full well there are boys who would find that difficult. It's all too easy to get addicted.

People wonder why gambling is such an issue in football, but when there's so much money swilling around, problems are inevitable. As footballers we're egotistical, we're competitive. We want to outdo one another. If we're playing poker, the stakes might start off at £20. Then someone will say, 'Forget that! I want it to be a £100!' Before you know it, you're talking £300. Five minutes later it's a grand. Then 10 grand. And so on and so on and so on. I've heard about the England boys losing two to three hundred grand on games of Uno. One of them won a million quid – on Uno! People will ask, 'How can that possibly be?' But when ego, competitiveness and money is thrown into the mix, silly things start to happen. You're talking about a bunch of people who won't back down. It doesn't matter what they're doing, they want to do it better than the person next to them. I'm the same. In football, I'm most competitive against myself, constantly wanting to do better. But in any other walk of life, if there's a game, me versus you, I'm wanting to get one over you in any way, shape, or form. I can be playing games at home with my kids and I'll still be doing my best to win. Footballers need to be competitive. Of course they do. But there's a danger side. There's a point in life where it needs to stop. The alternative is simple – addiction. I've never met anyone who's let gambling take over their life, but I do know people who've found it hard to leave it alone, who genuinely believe it's a way to make money, or get stuck in a cycle of losing money and trying to win it back. That might happen once or twice, but everyone knows that in gambling, the house always wins.

High-profile ex-footballers like Paul Merson and Tony Adams raised awareness of addiction issues in terms of alcohol, gambling and cocaine, but there's always something else around the corner. The addiction I've seen most as a footballer is sleeping pills. Sometimes, as you might expect, that's because players can struggle to sleep and are desperate to get a good night's rest before a game. But more recently I've also seen them taking 'sleepers' on nights out. Drinking on top of sleeping pills gives them a feeling of being in a hypnotic state. It's a way round the rules surrounding drugs. Obviously, players can't take cocaine or other banned substances, but if they take sleepers with alcohol, and then force themselves to stay awake, they can still find that way of zoning out without breaking the rules. Club doctors, unaware that players are abusing these pills, innocently prescribe them to footballers. But they only give a few days' worth. What happens then is that, through friends or contacts, players find their own supply. Easy access only makes the problem worse.

The PFA increasingly sends addiction experts into clubs to deliver advice and support to players. They offer rehabilitation services through Tony Adams' Sporting Chance Clinic. When I started out those things never existed, but they absolutely need to because footballers are subject to the same temptations as anyone else. At parties or in nightclubs there are bound to be people with cocaine and other substances. I've never taken drugs in my life, but I have been offered coke on a night out. A girl I was talking to just came out with it. 'Would you like some?' 'Er, no thank you!' But when a player's guard is down, or they've had too much to drink, it's easy to see how it could happen. Nowadays, that player will be caught. Footballers are routinely subjected to drug tests, sometimes saliva, sometimes blood, sometimes hair. The FA can test players anytime, any place, including after a game, at a training session, or at home, without advance notice, multiple times during a season. Refuse and it's a four-year suspension. When I was around the England squad, tests noticeably increased. On a single day I got tested at the training ground and then later at my house. Playing for Jamaica was different again. So much testing. At one stage during the Concacaf Gold Cup, the competition for North American, Caribbean and Central American teams, I got tested by FIFA every single game.

You might ask why so many Premier League footballers make what appear to be bad decisions. Actually, the vast majority don't. But even those who shun the darker elements are subject to expectations that are unreal compared to normal life. Thing is, the pressure as a Premier League footballer isn't just to play like a Premier League footballer, it's to *act* like a Premier League footballer. That means the big house and the impressive car. It means the latest designer gear and the luxury holidays. It means the jewellery and the watches. It goes on and on. What I'm saying is, yes, the money's big, but so's the expenditure, and it's only going one way – up. The more money a player makes, the bigger the person they want to look, and so the already supersized car and multi-bedroomed house just keep getting bigger and bigger, as does all the rest of it. I know, because I've been that person. I've felt that pressure to look and act a certain way. I didn't have to do any of it. Of course I didn't. But it's hard to know what to do. While you often hear people talking about how much footballers splurge on cars and property, I expect those same people would have plenty to say if that same player was on 200 grand a week and living in a two-up, two down with a second-hand Dacia sat outside. See what I mean? You can't really win.

I'm not expecting anyone to get the violins out, but being a footballer with money is a double-edged sword. Not only is your cash going on all the stuff you might expect, but there's a whole load of other expectations, some of which can be incredibly difficult to deal with. Family relationships especially can very easily be damaged. The sudden presence of money can cause fallouts. As a footballer it's not hard to start feeling that the only reason some people are calling you is because they want something. There's been times when I've seen a name pop up on my phone and thought, *I know what they want.* I've had to say, 'Why do you only call me when you need something? How about you call and ask me if I'm all right?' I've fallen out with people over it. The accusation you then get is, 'You've changed. You've gone big-time.' A better reaction would be to consider their own actions; what they've done to cause the situation, to make you feel hurt.

Predators, meanwhile, lurk round every corner. Money is a magnet for those who might not have a player's best interests at heart. It brings attention. You need to know who to trust. The shortness of their career means footballers are liable to try to make an easy buck elsewhere. Often that means being lured into dodgy investments, putting their trust in asset management companies that promise the Earth only for the whole thing to backfire. I've seen it happen where those kinds of businesses go into administration and the player loses a massive amount. The statistics around Premier League players who end up going bankrupt after being badly advised are insane. But this is what happens when there's money in the air. People appear out of the woodwork promising everything, only for the reality to end up being a complete disaster. These days players are more likely to be introduced by their club to people who'll help them to look after their money, but when I signed for West Ham it was on me to find a financial advisor. In recent years, understanding the need for long-term security, I've invested in property, a relatively safe place to put my money. I've seen too many players make the same old mistakes taking unnecessary risks.

In the face of so many financial pitfalls, the best mindset would be to think, *OK, I'm going to live as normal a life as possible and stack the money up for the rest of my life.* It was a lesson I learned late in my career. You need to block out the voices that don't matter. Meanwhile, I can guarantee there are plenty of players setting out on their own journey about to make exactly the same mistakes as I did. I've seen it with my own eyes – youngsters who've had their first pay cheque, £500 a week, and gone out and bought a two-grand designer bag. All because they want to look the part. Inevitably, I think back to my old self. My first properly extravagant purchase was a Mercedes ML. I was 21 and on £1,000 a week. The car cost £60,000. The payment was £700 a month. At the same time, among a few other pretty hefty direct debits, I was renting a big house. It took an accountant to point something out to that 21-year-old me. 'Your outgoings are more than you've got coming in.' I was like, 'What are you talking about?' He sat down with me and showed me exactly the mess I was getting myself in. I was only managing to get by that month because of how the direct debits were scheduled.

When you're younger, it's only natural to follow the example of what you see around you. But in the end, a lot can be gained from not caring about other people's opinions. It's more important to be content with your true self. I always try to be nothing but myself. As soon as you start being fake, you lose who you are. If you feel you don't need a big house to be happy, then live in a little apartment. It's your choice. Your happiness. Look at Jay-Z. When he was worth $1 million, he had all the big chains, the watches, the diamonds he could buy. Now he's worth $2 billion and all he wears is black tracksuit bottoms and a T-shirt. Only every now and then do you see him in designer gear. I see that with a lot of billionaires – not flashy, just wearing basic clothes. It's all about finding that comfort within yourself. That's what I've tried to do. When I was growing up, I always felt I needed money to be happy – that's what tends to happen when you don't have very much of it! – but over time I've come to see that's not the case. You might say that's easy for a footballer to say. I get that. We're not exactly struggling on the minimum wage. And weirdly, the more money footballers make, the more stuff we get for free. I've had clothes, shares in businesses, high-end cars at 50 per cent of the price. But trust me, I've seen the problems that chasing money brings as well as the good stuff too.

I don't want my kids following in those footsteps. It's something I'm trying to teach them. It's good to have objectives, good to be driven, because it helps you make some meaning of your life. But the money that can come with ambition doesn't help you be happy. Happiness doesn't come from external things. You won't find it in a card game any more than you'll find it in a designer shop in the West End. Buying something might make you feel a moment of satisfaction, but happiness should be in your heart. If my children grow up with that understanding, I'm confident they'll be happy. Same as I'll be happy knowing I've employed my money wisely, and so can help my kids over the long-term, not just for the short period of my career. If they want to go to university, or build a career, I can be there for them. That's important to me, and it's important to a lot of footballers. It's just that, amid all the pictures of footballers' mansions, and them falling out of nightclubs, you don't hear about it.

In football, money dominates the narrative. It's at the heart of so many discussions: how much a player earns, how much they cost, their sell-on fee, sponsorship deals, this, that, everything. It's a subject that's unavoidable, so I won't avoid it here. What I will say, though, is that what I reveal in the next chapter doesn't define me. I'm neither a price tag nor a figure on a bank statement. I'm me, and as such I only ever wanted one thing – to be paid what I was worth. That, it turned out, would be a battle I had annually with West Ham.

TEN
CONTRACTS

My agent is fuming with me. I'm signing for West Ham, even though they've offered me a poor contract. The appeal is the security of a four-year deal. But he's having none of it. 'No way are you signing that!' He thinks I should put pen to paper on two years at the most.

I stick to my guns. 'What happens if I hardly play this year, or get a bad injury? What happens then?'

'Trust me,' he tells me. 'Whatever happens, I will get you a deal.'

But I see signing a short contract as a risk. I didn't have money growing up, and, while it's not the best contract in the world, now I'll be on £20,000 a week. A million pounds a year! When you've fought and fought to get to the pinnacle of English football, that's a pretty big deal.

*'I just want to get to 25 grand a week,' I tell him.
'If I get to 25 grand a week, I've made it. And
starting on 20 I'm nearly there, so I'll take the four
years.'*

*'Mike,' he tells me, 'I can get you more money than
this in two years' time in the Championship, let
alone the Premier League. Just sign for two years
and then you get to leave on a free.'*

I don't listen. Maybe I should.

My first professional contract, when I signed for Reading,
was for £500 a week. By the time I left three years later that
had increased to £3,000. Signing for Sheffield Wednesday in
2012 took me to £6,600, rising to £8,000 by the time I left
for Nottingham Forest, and a £6,000-a-week pay rise, in
2014. When I ran out in the Premier League a year later at
West Ham, I did so on that magic million pounds a year. Even
so, I could have got better wages in the Championship. There
were teams offering me nearly double what awaited me at
Upton Park. For me, though, it was a no-brainer. The Premier
League is the top of the pile. It was my dream to get there. I'd
never played football for money. I played because I loved the
game and wanted to see, ultimately, how far I could go. Other
players might have taken the cash, but I wasn't one of them.
To be honest, while it goes against the money-grabbing stereotype that exists in some people's minds, I think most players
would see it the way I did. In football, you don't chase the
money, you chase the opportunity. Take the opportunity,
perform well, and the money will come. West Ham was that

opportunity. I'd be on football's biggest stage. With all eyes on me.

That was the idea anyway. When, however, my contract came up for renewal at the end of that first season, West Ham proceeded to offer me a right-back's salary – because that's where Slaven Bilić had been using me most of the time – even though my rightful spot was as a winger. It was a small increase. I refused. I knew other attacking players were averaging 20–25 grand a week more than what they were offering me.

'No, I should be on what they're on.'

'But you played right-back last season.'

'Yes, as a favour!'

They weren't budging. In the end I signed the contract.

By the time that following season finished, however, I could go into the contract negotiations with an absolutely unbelievable record, scoring nine goals and being made Hammer of the Year by the West Ham United Supporters' Club. The club's response was to offer me the contract I'd wanted the year before. Again, I refused. 'Look,' I told them, 'all those boys who got this contract last year have moved up to another wage level.' They'd been given 15 grand more a week than I was going to get. 'That's what you should give me,' I argued. 'Why am I different?'

They wouldn't move. 'No. Forget the other players. This is where you are right now.'

My agent wasn't pleased. 'If you'd listened,' he told me, 'you'd be on a free right now and I could be talking to top-four clubs. You f***ed us both!' He was right. Thankfully, we've been mates since we were kids. We can both laugh at this stuff. And I don't blame myself for picking security over risk. I've got responsibilities in life and they'll always come first. I also remember my path to the top. When I set out as a pro, the giddy heights of million-pound contracts seemed a long, long way away. Even so, I was pissed off with West Ham's attitude. After such a great season, and with the promise of more to come, I didn't think it unreasonable to expect better money.

As a player, what you really need at a time like this is a few other clubs knocking on the door, a bit of outside noise, some media speculation. 'Is he going here? Is he going there? Such and such a club is looking at him.' But you also need at least one bid to go in. As soon as your club knows you're genuinely wanted, your hand is strengthened massively. Speculation is one thing, firm interest something else entirely. Now the club's like, 'Oh shit. Right, we'd better find out what stage the talks are at.' They start to think about what they need to do to keep you. The threat of losing a key asset tends to concentrate minds and open wallets. But that wasn't happening. In the end, I had no choice but to accept their offer.

Another year on and I couldn't help noticing that the club was bringing in new players in my position – on the money I'd asked for! *OK*, I thought, *now they really are taking the piss.* They offered me the same. You might think I'd be happy. But remember, when I joined West Ham, I was on less than other people. Now, as an established player, I was expected to accept being on the same as the new arrivals. 'I know what you're giving them,' I told them, 'and it follows that I should be on more.' Once more, they refused. It was so frustrating. Time and again I ended up signing the contract I should have been on the previous year. The penultimate contract would be the biggest kick in the balls. Again, I signed, only for them to bring another player in on £40,000 a week – that's two million a year – which was more than me, and again in my position! A year later when I asked for a rise, I got the football club version of 'talk to the hand'. 'We're trying to cut the budget.' And then, as ever, they brought in another striker on more money. In the end, that person hardly played. He was sat on his backside on more money than me while I played game after game – another recurring feature of my time at West Ham. Seeing strikers come in, not perform as the manager had hoped, and leave with their pockets full of money was my version of Groundhog Day.

While in the early years I was hamstrung by that initial contract, all through my career at West Ham I felt disrespected. It seemed to me that whatever I did for the club, they didn't see it. My agent would go head-to-head with David Sullivan. More often than not the chairman wouldn't move on the contract and so I'd end up going in to see David myself. Those conversations were always civilised and good-humoured and usually ended up with him increasing the offer a little bit, although still nowhere near what I was hoping for.

I should say at this point that I do have a great agent. In fact, Mike Appiason's the thing I'm most grateful for in my career. I signed with him when I was 19, and my only regret is that I didn't do it earlier. When I was at Tooting & Mitcham, a different agent signed me. Signing for Reading, I was waiting for him to bring in the sponsorship deals I needed – boots, that kind of thing – but he did none of it. Other than signing contracts, I never heard from him. I was like, *I thought they did more than this!* When Mike approached me, he asked, 'What does your agent do for you?' 'He does my contracts,' I replied. 'No,' he said, 'I mean what does he really do? He should be doing all sorts of deals for you to justify the money you're paying him.'

I tried to terminate the contract with my existing agent, but he didn't return my calls. The next year I signed for Sheffield Wednesday, all sorted out by Mike and his boss at the time, Marion, with whom I also had a great relationship. I then got a letter from my former agent saying he was entitled to his money from the deal. Because he didn't terminate the contract when I asked, there were still 16 days on it to run when I signed at Hillsborough. I was obliged to pay him accordingly.

Footballers complain about agents a lot, and I know what it's like to have one who, I felt, didn't work hard enough for me. That's why I always say one of my best decisions in football is to have an agent I can rely on, someone who, whether it's to my face, or behind my back, is saying the same thing. Mine and Mike's relationship is unbelievable.

Though loyalty in football is often questioned, it's actually preferable for players to change clubs rather than remain with one team. Move and you make more money. Your new club is paying for you at a premium price. Stay where you are and you lose value. You're contracted for a certain number of years, and the club takes advantage of it. A new player, on the other hand, is fresh and exciting. 'Come to us! Here! Take the money!' Stay at a club for 10 years like I did and you see that discrepancy, that inequality, happen before your eyes. You won't ever get paid like the players coming through the door. Even when those players don't perform, it makes no difference. You're kept on your level and that's that.

There were times when I came close to leaving West Ham. Most summers the club would tell me I wasn't for sale, but there were a couple of occasions when they said I could leave. Me and my agent would do all the work, get a few clubs interested, and then inevitably West Ham would change their mind. The summer of 2023 was the closest I ever came to going. There was real interest from another Premier League side willing to pay what West Ham wanted. Of course, when the season then started and I was once again putting the ball in the back of the net, the club pulled the offer away from me. It happens to players. They put their talents on display and suddenly the club they're at remembers why they're such a big part of the side. There were other potential opportunities – considering I was there 10 years there were bound to be – but it seemed that every time there was interest, I got injured. And, while it sounds crazy, every time that happened I saw it as a signal that I wasn't meant to leave. That wasn't a bind, because, as I've said, I always enjoyed playing for West Ham. The more I was there the more it became my team. But the club definitely did well out of the fact I stayed.

The way contract negotiations are conducted in a cloak-and-dagger secrecy works in a club's favour. Because there's so little actual information about what teammates are earning, it makes it hard for players to compare contracts and, if they suspect they're being sold short, ask for more. Go to the board and say, 'You need to pay me the same as him,' and they'll just turn round and say, 'What makes you think he's on that?' They'll never point-blank answer the question. They can always get around it. A lot of the time clubs will tell players, 'Keep quiet about what you're on – don't tell the others.' They claim that players revealing their wages will cause unrest. That's not actually true. Money won't cause an issue in the dressing room, but it will cause an issue between players and owners, because footballers, like everyone else, need to feel they're being paid what they deserve. When that doesn't happen, some kind of resentment is inevitable. 'I'm here doing my job, doing my best for your club, and you're not paying me what I'm worth.'

In an ideal world everyone would be paid what they're worth, but football clubs are far from ideal worlds. They're personal empires run by a small number of people who keep a very tight grip on the purse strings. As a result, there's always a lot of speculation about what people are earning, but very few real facts. Everything's based on hearsay. Footballers, like anyone else, don't tend to go round mouthing off about what they earn. In fact, no matter where the discussion might go in the dressing room or team bus, they will always keep it to themselves. That's not hard to do. Let's face it, in the Premier League everyone's on so much money that no matter what car they turn up in for training, chrome Lamborghini or whatever, no matter what house they buy, it can never be seen as an indication of them being on more money than anyone else. What does tend to happen is that over time you'll maybe hear a few whispers, or someone will let something slip and you'll start to form a rough idea of what a teammate is on. Even then, though, you're still employing a fair amount of guesswork.

What is for sure is that wages have risen massively since I first joined West Ham in 2015. I can guarantee that now, in the mid-2020s, half the Premier League will be paying players more than £100,000 a week. The average weekly wage among all players will be £50,000–£70,000. And within that average there'll be guys on 400 grand a week plus. On top of that comes signing-on fees, appearance money and bonuses. Finish a certain place in the league and you get a certain amount. Defenders get bonuses for clean sheets, same as attackers get bonuses for goals. Stay at a club for a certain length of time and you'll get a loyalty bonus. Not that all 'extras' come through to the players. West Ham collected £4.3 million when we won the Europa Conference League. We got 15 per cent of the pot while the club took 85 per cent. It's understandable they should get the majority – they organised the flights and accommodation, etc – but we were the ones playing the games. The fact that we got so little was, to my mind, outrageous. They didn't even give us a memento of the victory. We couldn't believe it. 'Hang on, West Ham has won nothing in 48 years and you're not going to give us a single thing, not a little trophy each or nothing?'

All any footballer wants is to be treated fairly by their club. But, as I was about to find out in the starkest of ways, fairness and football rarely go hand in hand.

ELEVEN
CRASH

'*Have you heard about Diogo?*'

I'm doing some rehab work in Manchester, warming up on the exercise bike, when the physio asks the question.

'*No,*' *I reply.*

'*He's died.*'

'*What?*'

'*Diogo Jota – he's died in a car crash.*'

My whole body starts to shake. My eyes fill with water. I try to compose myself, but my body carries on trembling for the next 30 minutes.

All I want to do is see his car. I have to see the state it's in. I need to know if it's worse than mine.

To understand how I've survived and he's had his life taken away from him.

I search online for photos. It's two days before I find any. When, finally, I see those pictures, see how

badly smashed up Diogo's car is, it isn't a relief. I'm
too full of disbelief to feel like that. All I can think is
HOW? How, seven months after me nearly dying in
a car crash, can another Premier League striker die
like that?

I don't remember my own crash.

What I do know of that stormy December Saturday in 2024 is that, setting out to training ahead of West Ham's game at Wolves on the Monday, my plan had been to take the other car, a much sturdier Porsche Panamera. But the kids' schoolbags were in the Porsche and, when my partner asked me to get them out before setting off, I couldn't be bothered. It was one of those snap decisions. 'You know what? It's fine. I'll just take the Ferrari.' I know, lazy, right? And so I took the FF I'd bought just a few weeks before. FF stands for Ferrari Four. Unusually for a supercar, it's a four-seater. It was one of my dream cars, but I'd been on the verge of giving it back to the dealership. The rear end kept swinging out on me. Me and that car just never got on. In all honesty, I didn't really trust it. I didn't feel safe in it. A warning, perhaps, of what was to come.

I made it to West Ham's Rush Green training ground OK, went through various routines, and was heading home down a tree-lined road in Theydon Bois, near Epping, when … BLANK. Your guess is as good as mine. Weirdly, three or four months later, I began having a repetitive dream. I'm driving along when a white van veers across to my side of the road. I swerve, lose control of the car, and everything goes black. Is that what happened? I don't know. It was an incredibly windy day and it's perfectly possible that a van could have been pushed on to my side of the road. Or is that just my mind playing tricks on me? I guess we'll never know. Either way the Ferrari, with me in it, careered off the carriageway and ended up wrapped round a tree.

Forty-five minutes I was in that wreckage. Newspaper reports said I was found in the passenger seat, but actually I was sprawled in the back with my right leg between the front seats. I can't comprehend how I got there. People say I must have flipped out of the driver's seat, and that's what saved my life, but that can't be the case because one thing I can say for definite is that I had my seatbelt on. I always do. The beeping noises that modern cars make to remind the driver to buckle up irritate me too much not to. More likely that I unclipped the belt and then tried to save myself by crawling out of the car on my own. Sounds mad, but when I was a kid there was a certain spot on my knee which, if it took a hit, would make my whole leg go dead. Every time that happened I'd fall to the ground and drag myself along, like an army crawl, moaning with the pain. It was pretty horrible, and at the time felt like it lasted about five minutes, although I'm sure it would really have been no more than 20 seconds. I wonder if that's what I was doing in the car. A distant memory of that experience as a kid kicked in and I was trying to get my leg into a comfortable position. Again, no-one, me included, will ever know.

Apparently, I was awake the whole time I was trapped in that heap of smoking metal. According to a passing dog-walker I was saying the same few things over and over.

'Where am I?' 'What's going on?' 'What car am I in?' When, a few months later, I had the privilege of being able to meet and thank the paramedics who helped to save my life, they also told me I was vocal throughout. They were trying to keep me conscious, and so, having twigged I was a footballer – a big clue was the West Ham shirt with 'ANTONIO' emblazoned on it lying in the passenger footwell – they were talking to me about the game, my career, that kind of stuff. Again I kept repeating myself, which is quite common, or so I've since learned, when someone's hit their head. Not that it mattered. They didn't really care what I was saying. It was obvious to them that I was badly injured. My right leg was shattered and I was clearly in a lot of pain. The fact I was awake and talking did at least offer some reassurance.

Normally, with a lot of busy roads between me and the big city hospitals, it would have been an air ambulance job, but the weather meant that wasn't an option. From my position on the back seat, I was slid out on a board, on to a trolley, into an ambulance and blue-lighted to the Royal London in Whitechapel.

Two days later, I consciously re-entered my own life. In that time, I'd gone under the knife. Scans showed my femur was completely shattered in four places and surgeons knitted the bone back together with bolts and screws. Don't ask me how, but all that was done with keyhole surgery. The medical profession are the ones performing miracles every week, not footballers.

I was on morphine for three or four days. I don't mind admitting I was pressing that pain relief button again and again. Each hit felt so good. Lying in that hospital bed, as bit by bit I finally started to piece together what had happened, the realisation hit home like a hammer blow. I'd been in the kind of accident where people often don't come out alive, a suspicion confirmed when I asked my family to show me pictures of the car. I wasn't totally sure whether I wanted to see those images or not. When, finally, I brought myself to look, I had only one thought. *Oh! My! God!*

At that point, I didn't know whether I'd step on to a football pitch ever again. My career, which I'd worked so hard for, was hanging in the balance. But I also knew that in so many ways I'd been incredibly lucky. *I might have died and never seen my children again.* Tears filled my eyes. The thought was almost impossible to bear. That was by far the most difficult part of the whole experience, thinking I might not have been there for them anymore. Thankfully, I was able to turn that emotion around and see my survival for what it truly was – a second chance. That went for my football career too. The surgeon told me the operation had gone well, and that, while my leg had been a mess, when all this was over, 'You will be playing football again.' To hear those words was amazing. They gave me a massive boost.

I soon came to see that, in so many ways, my experience of the accident was a lot better than for those around me. Even though I was in it, I didn't live the crash because I couldn't remember anything about it. For everyone else, on the other hand, it was a living nightmare. I was actually talking to my sister on the hands-free minutes before the collision. In fact, I'd spoken to a few people, family and friends, while I was on my way home that day. And then the next thing they knew they were hearing I'd been in a terrible car crash. They were all like, 'What? How? No way! I've literally just spoken to him.' Frantically, they were calling me, their panic worsening when they couldn't get through, as my phone had remained in the car. It's horrible to think how terrified everyone must have been. Thankfully, they were told by the emergency services that early indications were I was going to be all right. But that wasn't the same for everyone. I heard later that when the news of my accident was broken to the West Ham boys, a few of them were in tears. In those first few hours they had no information whatsoever. They were looking on social media for updates. What they found was a whole load of grim speculation, with people saying, 'It's been confirmed! He's dead!' There were a few hours when a lot of people, them included, genuinely thought I was gone. Only later did they find out I was in hospital. Yes, badly injured. But alive.

In the days after the crash a lot of those West Ham boys, including Aaron Cresswell, Danny Ings, Vladimír Coufal and Tomáš Souček came to see me. Also among them was Niclas Füllkrug. I found that particularly moving. Niclas had only signed in August. He'd only known me four months and yet word was he was in tears when he heard what had happened. Manager Julen Lopetegui and vice-chairman Karren Brady arrived too. The response was incredible. On top of their visits, I had loads of messages from players, both privately and on social media. Declan Rice, a one-time Hammers favourite who'd gone on to great things at Arsenal, posted on his Instagram, 'Thinking of you and your family, brother. Prayers to all of you.' At that time everyone at West Ham and beyond showed me so much love, and it helped me massively. Like club captain Jarrod Bowen said at the time, 'Life is bigger than football sometimes.'

I watched that Monday night Wolves game, the one I'd been training for, from my hospital bed. When my teammates ran out on to the pitch in shirts bearing my name and number, it made me feel so emotional. At one of the lowest points of my life, and with my entire football future in doubt, it was a gesture of solidarity I hugely appreciated. And that wasn't the end of it. When Tomáš scored in the second half, he dedicated his goal to me by holding up nine fingers. Off the pitch, meanwhile, throughout the entire game the fans were singing 'Antonio! Antonio!' over and over. That wasn't just the Wolves match. Every game I watched over the next few weeks my name was being chanted from the stands. Gifts and cards from supporters arrived all the time, part of a deluge of good-will from across the world. At Marseille, the weekend after, fans held up an England flag with 'Antonio 9', 'WHU' and 'Marseille' on it. Amazing! The outpouring of caring and concern really touched me. It was that thing you hear about in times of difficulty, the football community coming together. I like to think I'm not someone who fans of any club have ever really hated. I hope they see me as someone who's happy just being himself. I also think fans like players who graft. I might not be the prettiest-looking footballer, but I definitely put in the hard yards, and I'm effective. Maybe also, because of the unconventional way I climbed to the top of the tree, they even see a bit of themselves in me. 'You know what? That could have been me!' sort of thing.

One way or another, there was a lot of emotion flying around in those early days. Some light relief came when I was visited by one of my best and oldest mates. Matty was sitting, chatting to me, when, all of a sudden, I had a desperate need for the toilet. Like a *really desperate* need. I managed to shuffle in there on some crutches but then found I couldn't quite sit down properly. Because of the operation, my right leg was in a weird position. No matter what I tried I just couldn't get comfortable. 'Matty!' I was moaning and groaning with the pain. 'You're going to have to come in and hold my leg.' And that's what he did. The poor bloke had to wipe my arse and everything. 'We can never speak of this!' he told me. So, instead I've put it in my book. Matty, what happened that day really did redefine friendship!

You can't beat honesty between friends. My agent Mike has known me since I was a kid – we actually used to play together at Tooting & Mitcham – and is like a brother to me, a closeness which maybe explains why, when he came into my room, his first words to me were the incredibly sympathetic, 'You f***ing idiot!'

Mike was having a laugh, but some of what happened around that time was mad. I had talkSPORT presenter Jim White call me after just a few days in hospital and try to put me on air. There I am sat in hospital and he tried to put me on the radio.

After five days in the Royal London, West Ham paid for me to move to the Cromwell, a private hospital in South

Kensington, where I could be more comfortable in my recovery. Aged 34, with a shattered femur, I'm sure some players would have lain back in that hospital bed and accepted that the moment of retirement had arrived, ready or not. I never for one minute had that thought. The second I was told I could carry on, and at the same level I was at before, that was it. I was going to do whatever it took to reach the point where I was back again playing in front of those fans who'd showed me so much love. The words of the surgeon – his reassurance that I'd be able to walk, then run, then, finally, play the game I adored – gave me the belief. The only question was how long I would need to get there.

I was under no illusion it was going to be easy. A couple of days after the operation, the doctors wanted me to stand up. The pain when my foot hit the floor was so excruciating that I actually screamed. It was clear from the start that if I was going to get back to where I once was, it was going to be a long and sometimes torturous road. The operation was only the beginning. Mending the leg was one thing; making it work again and remember what it had once been, entirely another. It was going to be a massive challenge.

The first few weeks were a case of simply trying to walk again, limping around, using crutches and a frame. Initially, I'd been told not to put any weight on the leg for three months, but another specialist said doing so would be beneficial, and so that's exactly what I started doing. The estimate was that it would take anywhere between six and 12 months for it to get anywhere near back to normal. I was determined that timeframe would be nearer six than 12. I was fit, I was strong and I was determined. I knew, if I gave my rehab absolutely everything I had, I could do it.

If the physical side of the recovery was hard, the mental side was doubly so. One occasion, about 10 days into my recovery, particularly sticks in my mind. The day started well. I was joking around with everyone, feeling pretty happy – possibly because of the morphine I was on! – and then in came the physio. While obviously I could hardly lift my leg at that point, I'd been doing well, bit by bit building up my strength. Now the physio wanted me to push on. 'We're going to carry on from yesterday and see if we can do a bit better.' Fine by me. I wanted to improve as quickly as I could. Except this day my leg seemed worse. Way worse. I could barely move it. Couldn't do even the most straightforward things.

'What's the matter?' she asked. 'Is everything OK?'

'I don't know. I don't understand what's going on. Nothing's working today.' As I was saying the words I could feel myself getting emotional. The physio must have sensed it. 'No problem. Let's leave it for today.'

The second she left the room I burst into tears. Crying, sobbing, like a child. I just couldn't stop.

My brother John phoned. As ever, he was totally in tune with me. He knew how hard everything was for me at that stage. The day before, with the aid of a walking frame, I'd got out of bed to go to the toilet. As I came back, I was physically shaking, shouting in agony. 'Oh my God! Help me into the bed! Get me in the bed now! Quick! Hurry up!' My leg was screaming. I was sweating, desperate to get some relief from the pain. It was the first time he'd seen me struggle like that.

Every other time he'd visited I'd been sat on the bed joking around. Unsurprisingly, he got emotional, to the extent he actually started crying.

When John called the next day, he asked me straight. 'I know you're a joker. I know you like to play games, make people laugh, be upbeat with everything, but I want you to be real with me. Don't play no games with me. How are you?'

'Honestly,' I told him, 'I've been fine. I've had no problems whatsoever. But today you've called me on the one day when I'm down.' I could hardly speak because I was crying so much. 'I don't know why I feel this way.'

Afterwards, I called my therapist. She explained what was happening to me. 'You might not remember the accident,' she told me, 'but your body still has lots of trauma and emotion that it needs to get out of its system. That's exactly what's pouring out of you now.' The echoes of the crash were still inside me. My emotional state was a sign of my body trying to release that stress. It was obvious that I couldn't go through something as massive as that accident and have it not affect me, but even so my body's reaction came as a tremendous shock. It was something else I'd have to get used to.

I will always be grateful to those who kept my spirits up in those difficult days. Between physio sessions and visits by doctors, my family kept me good company, sitting around chatting and playing games. When the crash happened, my littlest kids were shielded from the truth. They never knew how bad it was. But my eldest, 13 at that point, was being shown photos of the car by other kids. Understandably, that shook him up, and so it was important that he came to see me in hospital and saw with his own eyes that, while I was battered and bruised, I was basically all right. When they went home, I'd work my way through box sets. Finally, I got to watch *Game of Thrones*! OK, Christmas Day wasn't the most fun I've ever had. Aside from an hour with the family, I spent it alone. But that was my choice. They would have stayed longer but I didn't feel it was fair that they should spend such a special day in a hospital. Anyway, as a footballer I was well used to disrupted Christmases. With three games between Boxing Day and New Year, it's part of the deal.

That's not to say I was happy in there. Footballers are like everyone else. We don't like hospitals. If we're in hospital, something has gone seriously wrong. We're either injured or we're having an operation to repair an injury. Like everyone else, we want to get out of there as soon as we can and get on with our lives. Remarkably, considering how bad the crash was, I was only in for 24 days, discharged on New Year's Eve, a time when your mind naturally starts thinking about the year just gone and what the next 12 months might bring. Except this year, I wasn't thinking forwards or backwards, I was just grateful to be alive. I put out a post on my Instagram that day. Every word of it came from the heart.

Every year around this time, I'm asked what I'm grateful for, and every year I've struggled to find the right words. But this year, I know exactly what I'm grateful for: being alive.

I want to take a moment to acknowledge something I've come to realise – I've spent so many years taking life for granted. I made plans for the next day, the next year, always assuming tomorrow was guaranteed. I've seen close friends pass away, witnessed others face near-death experiences, and even then, I didn't fully grasp just how precious life is.

What I've been through recently has opened my eyes. Life is fragile, and every single moment matters. I'm so grateful to God for giving me the strength to keep going and for allowing me to still be here.

To the emergency services, the NHS, the Air Ambulance, everyone at the Royal London and Cromwell hospitals and everyone from top to bottom at West Ham United FC, the medical team, the board, all of the staff, my teammates and the amazing West Ham fans, I honestly could not have got through this without you. Thank you from the bottom of my heart. To my loved ones who stood by my side throughout everything, I can't express how much you mean to me.

Lastly, to the whole football community, thank you for all the love and support you've shown me. It has truly meant the world. I love you all and I am endlessly grateful for every one of you. ❤

Happy New Year – and I'll be back on that pitch soon.

That message encompasses exactly how I've come to see the crash. Yes, it was a curse, but it was also a blessing. It gave me a focus I never quite knew existed. Life is for living – NOW. Don't put off until tomorrow what you can do today. Make sure you do everything you can to make yourself and those around you happy.

While my own mood was lifted significantly by starting the New Year back in the comfort of my own home, the recovery programme didn't feel any less testing. Gradually, I went from lifting the leg, to holding it up and building muscle memory and strength. Considering what the paramedics had found in that Ferrari, the fact I was walking after five weeks is little short of miraculous. By then I could lift 90 kg with the leg, which, pushing myself within the boundaries of what was sensible, I soon upped to more than 100. With the benefit of six rehab sessions a week, I then moved up to 130 kg. This with a limb that not so long ago had been in pieces. As hard as it was to make myself do it, I could also hop and land on the leg with all my weight. So much of my recovery was about mind over matter. Knowing it needed to protect me, my brain would be telling me I couldn't do something, and it took a huge amount of willpower to override that message. The payoff was that after each session my leg was dead for a few hours. Slowly it came back to life. And, over time, so did I.

As with any knockback in my career, I worked and worked. Hour after hour, day after day, in the gym. I'm not saying that was easy. It was another massive test of resilience. But the only time I ever considered the gut-wrenching possibility that

I might not play again was when a physio asked me if I had insurance cover for a career-ending injury. That sent my mind spinning off in all sorts of directions – what did he know that I didn't? As it turned out, he was just asking me the question. It was nothing to worry about.

Less than three months after leaving hospital, I was back on the pitch at the London Stadium. Not playing – that really would have been a miracle – but walking out before the game against Newcastle United to receive the love of the fans face-to-face. I knew it would be an emotional moment, and I'd braced myself for it, but nothing could prepare me for the sight of the Hammers faithful unfurling a massive banner stating 'Michail Antonio – our number 9'. There's something about fans connecting with you not just as footballer, but as a human being. For seeing you as flesh and blood, the same as them. If someone stopped me in the street and asked me how I was doing, it meant a lot. But for 62,000 people in the London Stadium to stand and applaud was something else. I turned to walk back down the tunnel just as the teams came out. I was determined inside that one day soon I'd be back with them.

Deepfelt emotion was my constant companion. When my birthday came round on 28 March, I heard a song, 'I'm Blessed', all about second chances and surviving. Straight away I burst into tears. I truly was blessed. I was lucky to be alive. Even writing about it now makes me feel emotional. The same thing happened another time when I heard Beyonce's 'I Was Here' where she sings about leaving an impact on the world before her life comes to an end. I'd heard it a lot of times and never really focused on the lyrics. But now, as I sat with my kids, it seemed like her words were aimed directly at me. I could see everything I, and they, could have lost. It was totally overwhelming. Life is something that can never be taken for granted. Anything can happen at any time. That's why I believe in living for the moment. At any point it can all be taken from you.

Certainly, if there's one thing a near-death experience does it's to concentrate the mind. The biggest thing I learned from the crash is that, while football matters, there's nothing more important than your health. It made me think about what I wanted to do with my life, the things I'd kept pushing back, things that might never have happened because I almost died. The fact I'd already been having therapy for a couple of years at that point was also massive. Had that not been the case, had I not had someone to talk to about my innermost thoughts and feelings, I'm not sure how I'd have processed the accident. Instead of coming to terms with almost dying, chances are I'd have pushed my feelings down and been angry or aggressive. But the reality is that since the accident I've been more emotional than at any point in my life – and I like it.

There were constant landmark moments, emotional and physical, throughout my recovery. Making the trip back to the training ground for the first time since that fateful day was one of them. To be there among the boys, even as a visitor, was amazing. By then I'd returned from a 12-day warm weather training programme in Dubai and was able to resume running. I didn't want to cause any setbacks, but if I could push myself then I would. I could feel myself getting stronger and stronger. I knew what I was capable of. I knew I could make it back.

The clouds were disappearing and the sun was beginning to shine once more. Or so I thought. Behind that sunlight, one hell of a storm was brewing.

TWELVE
PIECE OF MEAT

It almost – almost – made me laugh.

'So, for everything I've done at West Ham, everything I've achieved over the past 10 years, you're going to let a manager who's done nothing from the day he arrived treat me like this? And then you have a problem when I say clubs treat players like meat?'

They couldn't have better proved the exact point I was making.

West Ham didn't want me back.

Forget all the statements of support, the little clips of my recovery on their Instagram, the invite to walk out on to the pitch for the Newcastle game. It felt like a sham. I think they never had any intention of having me back. I believe it was all just a set-up to make them look good.

My contract was up for discussion at the end of the season, but from West Ham's point of view I was a dead man walking. They were never going to give me anything. The day when, five-and-a-half months after an accident that could have killed me, I returned to the club, not as a patient but as a footballer, should have been one of the most momentous of my life. Instead, it was made clear to me, in the most obvious and hurtful of ways, that I wasn't welcome. I wouldn't be allowed around the first team at the training ground; I'd do my fitness work separately. I could use the first-team changing facilities, but not the first-team gym. I could eat in the canteen with everyone else but obviously, having been made an outcast, I knew that would be awkward. In the end, I'd come in, do what I needed to do, and go home.

The attitude of the club came as a shock. I phoned the chairman David Sullivan. David's very down to earth, chilled out. We'd always got on really well, I was his signing after all, and we had a mutual respect for one another. But now there was a different tone to his voice. It was like something was going on that he couldn't tell me about. We'd always had a bit of banter about contracts. 'Give me this!' 'No, I'm not giving you that!' He always won, but the whole thing was done in a civil way. Now he felt distant, cold. I felt the same distance from Karren Brady, who again I'd always got on well with. Suddenly, something I'd been saying for years in interviews, that in many ways footballers are treated like pieces of meat, had become a very big deal. I didn't just pluck the phrase 'piece of meat' out of thin air. I chose it very deliberately. After all, there's not many other areas of life where people are bought and sold with them barely having a say in the process. We earn good money, but we live in a very controlled environment, and the minute we're seen as going off we're chucked out. I was being told that by saying such things I was being ungrateful and disrespectful. But I'd been on about this stuff in the media and on podcasts for years. How come it was a problem now?

Doubtless knowing how bad it would look if they ditched a long-serving player who'd nearly died, the club tried to make out they had actually offered me a deal. The situation really pissed me off. In the media, West Ham were making it look like one thing, a natural parting of the ways after a bit of a contract wrangle, when really it was something completely different.

I didn't hear it when it was broadcast, but when I was going back and forth with West Ham, Simon Jordan told talkSPORT, 'West Ham didn't crash his car, he did. He put himself in that situation.' When someone told me what he'd said, my first reaction was, 'Who's Simon Jordan?' I'd never heard of him. I didn't even know who he was (the former Crystal Palace owner, apparently). To me, it was a classic example of what you often hear in the media – someone saying something to get a bit of airtime.

I wasn't interested in clickbait comments. I wanted to speak to the people who mattered. I rang Brady. 'I can't believe you guys keep saying that you've offered me something when you haven't. Stop telling the press that's what happened. Stop trying to make out you guys are great, that you've done everything you can, when actually you've not offered me a single thing.'

I was so close to calling the press myself or at least putting it up on my socials. What I felt like saying at the time was: 'You know what? This club isn't telling the truth. They didn't offer me anything.' I chose to be more graceful. I could see only too well the way the wind was blowing. My plan instead was to sign for another club and show West Ham what they were missing out on; that this wasn't the end of me. I would come back somewhere else.

Maybe it was the prospect of some very bad publicity that sparked the board into action. They came back to me with an offer to train and play with the Under-21s for six months. But, in my eyes, as the club's top Premier League goalscorer, a loyal servant for 10 whole years, and with a medical diagnosis that I could be as good as I was before, they were presenting me with something they must have known full well I was never going to accept. More than that, it felt like they were trying to embarrass and humiliate me. I'd have been on less money than the kids around me. Despite having served the club for 10 years, I'd be playing alongside lads in their teens earning more. And anyway, playing with the Under-21s wasn't going to help me get another club. Who was going to see me? Also, as an overage player I was limited in how many times I could turn out for them. It was a contract that wouldn't aid me in any way, shape or form. My reaction was predictable. I had no choice but to call them up.

'You guys are taking the piss. If that's all you're going to offer, I'd rather have nothing. I'd sooner retire than sign a contract like that.'

It felt clear that Graham Potter was at the root of the club's abrupt change in attitude towards me. The former Chelsea and Brighton boss had been brought in after Julen Lopetegui was sacked in May. Our Portuguese manager getting the bullet was a blow. He liked me as a person, rated me as a player, and I had a good relationship with him. As soon as Potter came in, on the other hand, I was gone. Again and again he'd tell me, 'It's the chairman's decision whether he wants to give you a contract or not.' I'd ask the chairman, only to get the cold shoulder. Back to Potter I'd go. 'There you go. He's giving you nothing.' But of course, he was giving me nothing because Potter didn't want him to give me anything. Sullivan was doing what all good chairmen do – backing his manager. And in the meantime, that same manager was peddling this line about me being a negative influence.

It annoyed me so much. Yes, it can be humiliating for a player to end up training away from the first team. While I was being frozen out at West Ham, the same thing was happening to Raheem Sterling at Chelsea, even training alone at night at the Blues' Cobham training ground. Of course I'd rather have been with the first-team boys, and yes, I had to swallow my pride during what was an incredibly frustrating period for me, but I was also well aware that I might never have kicked a ball again in my life. Or even had a life. I was always trying to find the positives. It might not have been exactly what I wanted, but at the same time as building my fitness I was also enjoying helping out the younger players, especially the strikers and the wingers, giving them the benefit of my experience, showing them ways to improve. More than anything I was just happy to be out there enjoying what all my life I'd always loved doing. And yet here was this constant narrative being wheeled out: 'Michail's being negative.' None of them who spoke those words will ever know how hard I tried, in the most testing of circumstances, to be the exact opposite.

I'll always remember my last time at the training ground. I'd been in as usual with the Under-21s. Afterwards Josh Ewens, doing some fitness coaching, came across to me. 'Graham Potter wants to speak to you.' By then I wanted nothing to do with him. In fact, I distinctly remember my reply. 'Tell him to f*** off.'

I've known Josh a long time. I respect him and we get along well. 'If you want me to tell him that, I will,' he said. 'But I know you, Michail. You should think about it first. Maybe just hear what he's got to say.'

I considered his words. 'All right. No problem. Tell him I'll be there in 30 minutes.' I was happy to make Potter wait. No way was I going to be at his beck and call. I got showered and headed to his office. There was no 'How's it going?' or anything like that. He got straight down to it. 'I told you that I don't want people around the club behaving negatively.'

'Have I been negative?' I asked him. 'When you've seen me at the training ground, have I been negative in any way?'

'I've hardly seen you,' he replied.

'OK, well has anybody in or around the coaching staff said to you that I've been negative? Because I know for a fact I haven't. I know for a fact I've been around the boys, the new signings included, having a laugh and a joke with everybody. You might not know my character, but everybody in here knows how I am. I don't mope. I try to be positive and uplifting all the time.' I looked at him. 'You're doing bad enough without me throwing any shade around.'

'Well,' he said, 'we don't like the comments you're making in the press.'

'OK, what comments are they?'

'Like how clubs treat players. That's very negative.'

'But I've been saying that for years. I was saying it when I had my podcast. If you guys think it's negative, you need to look at yourselves. Because all the time I've been at the club, all the time I've had a contract, no-one's ever said nothing about it. Now I've almost died in a car crash and don't have a contract, you think it's negative. To me that means the only problem is your own guilt. Because otherwise what's changed? If you think me talking like that looks bad, it can only be because of what you've done.'

'Well,' he said, 'if you're going to be doing those types of things I don't think you should be coming to the training ground.'

I wasn't having that. 'And what about your duty of care to me?' I asked. 'You have a duty of care to help me get over my injury. So I don't care what you feel. I'm going to come in here, and I'm not going to be moody, because I'm not a moody person, and I'm going to do the work that needs to be done.'

Potter accused me of playing games and went back to telling me not to turn up at the training ground. 'I don't want anyone there who wants us to do badly.'

As someone who'd done nothing but try to bring success to the club, I felt that was a huge insult. 'Honestly,' I told him, 'I do not care about you in any way, shape or form. I have no emotion towards you. I have no connection to you. What I do care about are these boys and this club. I want them to do well at all times.'

I'd had enough. I walked out the room.

I understood only too well what Potter was doing. He didn't like a squad with a lot of senior boys. Towards the end of his disastrous nine-month reign at West Ham there was a lot of media chatter about him losing the dressing room. By the time he was sacked I'd left the club so it's hard for me to say whether that really was the case, but I'd seen with my own eyes the problems he was bringing on himself. To me, Potter was a manager with no balls. He didn't know how to deal with ego – how to deal with players who came back at him and said things he didn't agree with. While I was there, a couple of the older players pulled him up for being a hypocrite. Potter's mantra was, 'Train well and you'll get your opportunity.' But the team sheet never seemed to match his words. 'You say this, you say that,' they told him, 'but there's boys doing exactly what you said, performing great in training, and they're not starting on the weekend.' His reaction to that was, 'Get out of the room!' Which wasn't going to solve anything.

Potter's answer to being challenged was to bring in young players, who, not wanting to rock the boat early in their careers, are more likely to be 'yes' people. But getting rid of big personalities is problematic, because in a football club, especially one that's struggling, strong characters are exactly what you need. When you're battling on the pitch, it's those players who bring the team through the hard times. Off the pitch, meanwhile, they're vital for building team spirit. That's why Potter struggled at Chelsea, and that's why he struggled at West Ham. Potter needs to be at a club full of 19 and 20-year-olds who he can exert some control over.

Some people will say Potter was a victim of player power that got out of hand. But these older heads know what they're talking about. They've been playing for years. They know what to do. They know how to build unity. And that's exactly what was needed at those two big London clubs. When a manager is straining for results, he needs people pulling the boys together. When things get so bad that the players don't want to listen to the gaffer and don't trust him, someone in the dressing room has to do his job for him. That person can't be a member of the manager's staff in case they're seen as a mouthpiece. It needs to be a trusted player who's going to pull the boys together and get the job done. Instead, Potter waved goodbye to Aaron Cresswell (11 seasons at West Ham), Lukasz Fabianski (eight) and Vladimír Coufal (five) despite the feeling among a lot of the players and fans that they should get new deals. Edson Álvarez is another case in point. He might only have been at the club for two seasons, but he was a strong character, the captain of Mexico no less. Potter's response? Let him go.

No surprise then that he wanted rid of me too.

The irony was, of course, that I was in fact the biggest, most positive story they could have wished for – the club's record Premier League scorer returning to continue his love affair with West Ham after the car crash that should have killed him. Instead, they wanted to kick me out the door.

No way was the club going to change its mind. 'I'll stay until the end of the window,' I told them, 'by which time I'll most likely have signed for another club. Then I'll be gone.'

'That'll be best,' I was told, 'both for us and for you.'

'It won't be best for me,' I said, 'but it will be best for you.'

My agent thought about bringing in the PFA to help me fight my corner, potentially even sue the club. In the end, though, I didn't want the psychological burden, not to mention expense, of a legal case dragging on and on. These things can last for months, potentially even years. I wanted the positive focus of getting back into football.

And so that was that. After the window, I didn't go back. I never got a proper chance to say goodbye to the fans who I'd had such a fantastic relationship with for a decade. It was hurtful. How often do players stay with the same side for 10 years? I'd never supported a team in my life, but after so long at West Ham they'd become my club, and my kids' club too. Half the pictures I have of them are in West Ham gear. Imagine you've been somewhere that long and they treat you like that? Forget the football; they had a duty of care to me as a person. They didn't seem to care. I believe they saw the crash as an opportunity to get rid of me. In doing so, they also, contrary to the nonsense they were throwing my way, got rid of one of the most positive presences around the club and dressing room they'd ever had.

That's how I'll always look at it. The fans at West Ham were amazing, but the way the club treated me was unforgiveable. I'd done everything they'd ever wanted, played all over the pitch. And I wanted to give them more. I was still ambitious. I wanted to get to 100 Premier League goals, to cement the West Ham record. Usually, when a player says goodbye after such long and loyal service they'll be told, 'You'll always be welcome. Come back whenever you want.' They might even be offered some kind of ambassadorial role. They say there's no room for sentiment in football, but even if they no longer had belief in me, they could at least have brought me on at the end of a game; at least let me say goodbye to the fans and them say farewell to me. Not getting that opportunity affected me massively. It didn't need to be a league or cup game, it could have been a match of no importance whatsoever, pre-season, anything. The friendly against Lille at the London Stadium the week before the big kick-off in August would have been perfect. They could have given me five minutes – just five minutes – at the end. But it wasn't to be.

A couple of times, rather than let me play in the claret and blue for one last time, they talked about having me walk out on to the pitch ahead of a game, but it just didn't feel right. I didn't like either the sound or the look of it. Compared to actually playing, it felt hollow, insincere and meaningless. Was I really meant to walk out with a big smile on my face knowing the attitude of the people at the top of the club? There were so many opportunities for me to say farewell, and Potter point-blank refused. He didn't want me around and that was that. Fine. My view was I'd say my goodbyes when I came back with my new team. Walk round the pitch at the end of the game or something. I'd show the fans the respect they deserved even if the club couldn't extend that gesture to me.

At least I got a chance to say my goodbyes to the players. 'Look,' I told them, 'I'm not sure what's happening, but I might not be here on Monday. So let me just say goodbye to you guys.' The boys' comments were sympathetic. 'You should still be here.' 'I can't believe how they're treating you.' 'I can't believe they're not giving you another year.' Everyone I spoke to thought I'd at least have been given that option, because it happens all the time. Josh Dasilva at Brentford is a great example. After barely playing for two seasons due to significant injuries, the Bees were still keen to show him their support. The midfielder signed a new contract, with the option of a further year attached. Towards the end of his career, West Ham themselves gave club legend Mark Noble a one-year contract after a season when, understandably considering he was well into his thirties, his appearances had started to drop off. That's exactly what should have happened to a player who'd shown such commitment, such loyalty, to the West Ham cause. In my case, I was still starting games – same as I had every year since joining West Ham – when I had the crash. I would have started the match the Monday after. Was I really wrong to think the club would give me my year? Allow me the chance to come back and prove myself like I've seen so many other players do?

When, after 10 years at Newcastle, Jamaal Lascelles suffered an anterior cruciate ligament injury, ruling him out for six to nine months, his manager Eddie Howe didn't bin him off. He couldn't wait to tell anyone who'd listen what an important cog in the wheel the defender was, what a big role he played in the squad dynamic. When the Magpies won the Carabao Cup a year later, Jamaal was invited to lift the trophy at Wembley even though he hadn't played in the competition. So many clubs have given players contracts out of respect for their loyalty. The club I was at chose not to – with a player who very nearly died while wearing their shirt. People say to me it's heartless, and they're right. I used that exact same word when I spoke to Karren Brady for the final time.

There's a footnote to this sorry little story. A few months later I heard via the grapevine that the chairman had wanted to give me a deal, same with Aaron Cresswell. While we could still physically do it, he wanted to keep us at the club. Unfortunately, Potter didn't want us around, the chairman put his trust in him, and that was that. As a result, I'd spend months searching for another club. All because of a guy who had no connection with me, didn't care that I'd been at the club for 10 years, or what I'd achieved. I was left in limbo, the club was left in freefall, and the chairman was left getting dog's abuse.

Honestly, I love West Ham. I so wished it could have been different. West Ham was my life. I'd made 323 appearances, scored 83 goals and played in the team that won the club's first major trophy in almost half a century. I gave West Ham the best years of my playing career. But the truth was that none of it counted for anything. I was dead to them.

Meanwhile, West Ham stuck with Graham Potter – and look where it got them.

THIRTEEN
LONG WAY BACK

I'm in the bathtub in a hotel in the Bahamas. I've got YouTube up on my phone. But this isn't a football compilation I'm watching, or some bits of comedy. It's Mum's funeral. In my absence, it's been uploaded by my family.

My sister calls me at one point. My eyes are streaming as she tries to speak to me, to tell me how the day has gone.

The water starts off hot. By the end, it's gone cold around me.

I didn't want the end of my career to be a car crash. Literally, a car crash. But there were times when that really did appear to be the case.

While I was back training after five months, my leg was still quite stiff at that stage. However, as I began playing for West Ham's Under-21s I could feel myself gradually getting nearer and nearer to match fitness. I really did feel like I was getting back to the player I was before the accident. I was impressed with myself. For the first time in a while I was looking at myself as a footballer and thinking, *This is quality!* But more than anything I needed a new club. It's a strange feeling when three o'clock comes around on Saturday and you're not part of the big kick-off happening around the country. As a footballer, your whole week is based around playing on the weekend. From the day I signed my first professional contract at Reading I've always been in and around first-team football. Suddenly, I'd time-travelled back a decade-and-a-half and was training with the Under-21s with the odd match here and there. The sooner I signed for a club the better. I knew it and was determined to make it happen.

And then, on 12 July 2025, I was on a night out for my brother's birthday, everyone having a great time, when I got a phone call from my sister. 'Mum's in hospital. She's not breathing properly.' By the time I got there she was dead. My sister was holding her, distraught, wailing. I couldn't deal with it. I went for a walk, came back, was in the room for 10 seconds, and had to leave again. I tried one more time. My family even offered to let me have the room to myself. It didn't make any difference. I walked out and went home. I was in bed for three days. Just me there in a darkened room. That went against everything I am. I love to be very involved with my kids, but I needed that 'me' time. They kept coming in – 'Daddy, what's wrong?' – but I just didn't have the energy to be around them. Mum's death was devastating, another terrible moment in the most challenging few months of my life. If I thought going through my divorce was one of the hardest things I'd experience, I'd soon encounter challenges 100 times more difficult.

Mum dying hit me so much harder than Dad's death during lockdown five years earlier, two days after my 30th birthday. I was in Manchester when I got the call saying he was touch and go. Sadly, as with Mum, I couldn't get to him in time, but the crazy thing is that Dad's eyes were open when he passed. Only when I walked into the room did he shut them. It was like he was waiting for me to arrive. At that time, of course, because of Covid, no-one was meant to mix. No way were we going along with that. After the funeral, everyone got together to celebrate Dad's life. I did actually get Covid afterwards. I was shivering in bed for a while. To this day, I've still not dealt with the emotion of my dad passing, yet his loss didn't feel as heavy as Mum's. Part of that, I think, is because he was 20 years older than her. He was 58 when he had me, and I was used to him being ill in old age. That doesn't mean I've processed it. I'm a person who pushes things down and I've certainly done that with Dad. Even with therapy, and being able to let my emotions out more, I know I still haven't dealt with it properly. But Mum was the one who was really close to me. Growing up, she was my best friend, always encouraging me with my football. She might not have been into it herself, but that didn't matter. Right from the start she kept pushing me on. She always made sure I had the kit I needed and the time and opportunity to train. She really did believe in me, and I can thank her for everything I achieved. The only downside was the 'mother tax' she charged when I started a couple of part-time jobs. Unbelievable! She buried me each month. She knew I just wouldn't say no. How could I? I knew what she did was amazing. This strong, strong woman held down two jobs and looked after us all at the same time. Crazy. They don't make them like that anymore.

Mum was the dominant person in our family. Dad would only speak if necessary. If he felt the need, you knew you'd gone too far. Not that Mum needed her husband when it came to discipline. She could handle that well enough herself. She disciplined us through respect. To her dying day I respected her so much. And yet, as much as she was strict with me, she was also someone who I felt comfortable having conversations with. I don't know how common it is for mums and sons to be like this, but I could talk to her about anything – and I mean anything. One thing she never knew about, though, was my accident. At that point she'd been ill for several years, bedbound, needing dialysis and also suffering from slight dementia. She had enough to deal with without the stress of nearly losing me too. I didn't want to send her over the edge. I was her baby boy. Just hurting my ankle in a game would make her lose her head. Imagine someone telling her I'd almost died in a car crash. It would have been unbearable for her thinking of me lying in that hospital.

When Mum passed away I was full of emotion, crying all the time. But eventually I reached a point where I felt able to tell myself it was time to start getting back to normal. The funeral is the next natural step in coming to terms with the death of a loved-one, but, for various family reasons, the date kept getting moved back. For me that was difficult. The Jamaica football team wanted me with them for a short series of World Cup qualifiers. I desperately wanted Mum's funeral to have taken place by then, but the situation rumbled on and on until, in the end, I had an incredibly difficult decision to make. You might ask, 'What decision?' I'm sure most people would just assume I'd put the funeral first. But it's not as simple as that. I'm a footballer. That's how I make a living for me and my family. Going away with Jamaica was important. It was a chance to show the football world how far I'd progressed with my recovery since the crash. Turning out for West Ham's Under-21s, one week I'd be blowing after 30 minutes, the next I'd be playing for 70. By the time August came round my body was moving really well. Constantly, I was turning it over in my mind. 'Can I really miss Mum's funeral?' Eventually, I reached a conclusion. 'Looking after me is looking after my family.' I would go to the qualifiers. I'd miss that final goodbye.

I'm not saying it didn't burn me to make that choice, because it did, more than anyone can imagine, but at the time it made sense. A few weeks earlier the Jamaica manager, the ex-England boss Steve McClaren, had taken me out to America for the Concacaf Gold Cup and had given me some game time. In the training sessions I was stiff, even limping a little bit. After such a long time out, that was bound to happen. But in the actual games, when I was introduced from the bench late on, I was good. With a decent warm-up, and the added adrenalin boost of playing, I wasn't restricted in any way. However, when I went back out in September for the World Cup qualifiers, it was like none of that had happened. I ended up feeling like a spare part. Beforehand I'd said to McClaren, 'I don't mind if you don't call me up, but if you do then I want you to be open-minded about me. Don't take me out there and treat me like a lost cause.' Like I say, I'd shown in the previous games that I could play, I could move. McClaren did call me up, letting me know there was no guarantee of game time, but then in the training sessions he kept putting me out wide on the wing. Not only was I not getting game time, I couldn't even train in my position on the pitch. One time, I totally lost it, shouting and swearing at everyone. I was totally exasperated. I'd gone out there hoping to help get Jamaica to their first World Cup since 1998 and they were using me like a passenger. I was on the bench, but there was no way I was ever actually going to get on the field. I felt helpless, like an extra in the final scenes of my career.

So there I was, sat in the bath watching my mum's funeral take place 5,000 miles away without me. *Should I have been there?* The question went round and round in my head. Mum had been laid to rest. From that point of view, me physically being there didn't make much difference. But it was about how much difference it made to me. Through therapy I've come to see that while me not being at my mum's funeral might look a certain way to people on the outside, what matters is how I feel. My problem is, I don't know how I feel. I don't know whether I'm right or wrong. Should I have been there? Should I have not? I'm stuck in limbo. But at the same time, I know I did need to focus on me, because my future is my kids' future. There are people all around me I need to look after.

I didn't talk to anyone about the quandary, the mental turmoil, I was going through regarding going to Jamaica. As much as I'm an outgoing, bubbly person, I'm also someone who can easily be left alone. And so I dealt with my conflicted feelings in my own way and kept myself to myself, same as when I left the hospital alone the day Mum died while everyone else went to her house to mourn her. Anyone who knows me will say that's totally in keeping with who I am. They know I'm like that because that's how I've always been, right back to when I was a kid. When it comes to being able to share my big emotional moments, I'm very much a work in progress. Like I say, I've been encouraged to release that side of myself more, and I know for my own mental wellbeing that has to happen.

It was for my mental wellbeing too that I had to get back into football. Even if I had to drop down to a Championship club, I was determined not to allow my life as a footballer to end on that windswept December day. I refused to let it finish that way. Everything I'd done in my career, all I'd been through to create a life in football for myself, no way could I let that happen. My career had to reach a natural full-stop with me hanging my boots up, not wrapping a car round a tree and being shown the door by West Ham. I was disappointed with having to leave the Hammers, so frustrated. But at the same time, I could tell myself, *I know what I'm doing. I know what my body is capable of. And I'll get the opportu-*

nity. I refused to call it a day on their terms. I had to go back out there and prove I had more left in me.

There was always hope. Just because I had no future at West Ham didn't mean I was dead in the water. My record spoke for itself. I knew I could still be a positive addition somewhere else. Even well into my thirties my intention was always to keep improving. My career trajectory up to my injury showed that was the case. I was still performing at a very high level. I've never stagnated as a footballer. I've always set myself targets. If you don't have something to aim for then what's the point? The only way is backwards – and I was never interested in that. But convincing other people to believe the same wouldn't be easy. Without the crash, I'd have walked through an open door into any number of clubs. Instead, because it was a femur break, I knew what those same clubs were thinking, *Is he actually going to be able to play again? He's not 25 anymore, he's 35. How's he going to heal?* On occasions, when me and my agent had discussions with clubs, they'd say it out loud. 'How's the leg? Tell us the truth.' We told them the truth. The leg was OK. I could play again. But no matter what we said, what evidence we provided, they just weren't sure.

Then Brentford came into the picture. They understood my pedigree and felt I still had something to offer in the Premier League. I was sure of that too. I knew people would doubt I could ever be the same player again, but all through my recovery I was 100 per cent confident that once I was playing, I'd get my sharpness back. I might have been 34 when I had the accident, but I had the fitness and speed of someone five years younger. Even in my final season, I was still one of the fastest at West Ham.

Naturally, Brentford weren't going to commit without looking at me. They wanted me to train with them over a prolonged period, essentially to trial for them, to show that I was physically fit. While that seemed a little bit over the top, Brentford definitely felt a good fit. They were an established Premier League club, were fairly near my home, and clearly were coming at it from the position of rating me. Over the course of those few days, they saw on the training pitch what I could do, and I was really enjoying myself too. This really did seem like the route back I'd been looking for. It was even pointed out to me that due to a quirk of the fixture list, in all probability my first game in Brentford colours would be back at the London Stadium. I might not have been in the team but I'd have been in the squad. Perfect. And then, on the day the Bees were going to sign me, with the pen as good as in my hand, my calf went. It was a grade three tear, the most severe type of calf injury, and exactly the kind of thing that happens when you're coming back from a long time out.

I couldn't help wondering if I'd been pushed too far too soon. Sat in the physio's room at Brentford I almost started crying. *How is this happening to me?* I actually said out loud, 'I think God just wants me to retire!' The Brentford boys were having none of it. 'No, no, I don't think your story's done.' I was heartened by their positivity and so instead of following my instinct and getting out of there as fast as possible, I stayed and did a bit of rehab. Afterwards, though, when I got home, I felt absolutely destroyed. All I could do was get in bed and let the tears come. I didn't leave those covers for the rest of the day. I was emotional. So emotional. Again, I had to fight that voice inside me. *F*** it! Just retire!* After everything that had happened – the accident, the recovery, leaving West Ham, the search for another club – I was *finally* getting back to playing football. Doing what I really wanted, to play again in the Premier League – and then right at the very last minute it had been torn away from me.

Eventually, I started to talk myself round. I didn't want to be negative about the situation. Truth is I could have died in that car crash. I could have lost a leg. So not getting a contract at West Ham or falling at the last fence at Brentford was far from the be-all and end-all. *You know what? I'm going to get myself right again.*

From the brink of the perfect comeback, I was plunged into yet more rehab. Initially that was with Brentford, but whereas a deal had felt guaranteed before, now it was more a case of doing my recovery work with them and seeing how it went before they made any kind of commitment. Sadly, that commitment wasn't forthcoming, although not for the want of trying. Later, when I'd recovered from the injury, I called Brentford up. 'You know what? I think we can do each other a favour. You want to sign a new striker in January and I need a bit of game time. Let's get this done.' It didn't happen, and so instead I started training with Leicester City.

While I knew I still had more to offer at the top level, I wasn't against the idea of dropping down into the Championship. All was looking good at the King Power, and I was set to sign a contract, only for their medical team to discover my calf hadn't healed properly. Once I'd got past that barrier, and the calf was OK, another hurdle appeared. West Ham had registered me as an Under-21s player, a technicality which meant I couldn't play for Leicester's first team. While the club were sorting this out with the EFL, I carried on training – and tore my hamstring. I pinned my hopes on it being a small grade one tear, because it wasn't too painful. Instead, it was a grade two – four to six weeks out. I couldn't believe it. Once more my footballing future had been snatched away at the last minute. It was Brentford all over again. I always tried to stay positive, because that's who I am, but there were times when I couldn't help thinking 2025 had been a dump of a year. First the calf injury, and now this, would mean I'd have been out for at least 14 months by the time I got back into football. That's a hell of a long time in professional sport.

But I can never be kept down for long. Overall, my mindset wasn't going to change. I still had the determination. I wasn't going to do what others might have done in the same situation: call it a day, take myself off on holiday and forget it all. Let's face it, 12 months previously I could barely get out of bed. I was in a much better place now. Not only were clubs showing an interest in me, but in the year after the crash I'd learned so much about myself and what I was capable of, on and off the field.

I was never going to just go away. Never going to sit still. This latest chapter of my career is one of many new and exciting adventures I'm setting out on which, weirdly, would never have happened without the accident. Who'd have thought nearly dying would give me so many new perspectives, so many new opportunities? Most of them I'm still coming to terms with. And one of the most spectacular of all is seeing the footballer's life through the opposite end of the lens.

FOURTEEN
PUNDITS

It's the opening weekend of the new season and I'm watching Manchester United play Arsenal at Old Trafford. The home team have gone in at the break 1–0 down. In the Sky studio, Roy Keane brands the United players 'weak and soft'.

This is 45 minutes into the season, and already United are being written off. Not that I'm surprised. I've seen it again and again. Because of who they are and what they achieved at the club, ex-United players feel justified in completely destroying the players who are there now.

I feel like saying to these pundits: 'Look! We understand what you've done and what you've achieved, but you need to let go. You need to remember that these players are human beings. They're young and impressionable. You need to give some positives, not just slate, slate, slate.'

A big deal for me during my recovery was starting out in a career on TV. It's been a long-held ambition of mine to become an established TV pundit and, eventually, presenter, but previously I'd never had the time to pursue it to any great degree. I'd done a couple of appearances on Sky's *Monday Night Football* show and *Match of the Day* on the BBC but really was just dipping my toes in at that stage. Only after the crash could I properly go for it, signing a contract with TNT. It helped that I'd already done multiple episodes of *The Footballer's Football Podcast* where I showed I knew plenty about the game and wasn't afraid to ruffle a few feathers if necessary. When, finally, my football career comes to an end, it's something I'm aiming to properly throw myself into. I'm not arrogant. There are skills to be learned, but if my football career has taught me one thing it's that if I put my mind to something I can, and will, do it. I also know I want to operate in a certain way. I've watched plenty of pundits down the years and, if I'm honest, haven't always liked what I've seen.

To me, the hardest team in England to play for is Manchester United, simply because so many former players have gone on to be high-profile pundits. I genuinely believe their constant negativity has affected the confidence, and therefore the performance, of some very good footballers. Only when those players leave do they start to rediscover the form that took them to Old Trafford in the first place. Being blamed by big-name players of the past, with the pressure that brings, can kill players off. Constant comparisons are as unkind as they are unhealthy. These pundits played in amazing United teams during the Red Devils' most successful ever period. But a football club can't always be like that. Football's like fashion, it goes through phases. Liverpool dominated football in the 1970s and 1980s and then didn't win the league for 30 years. Derby were a massive team and now they can't get out of the Championship. Bournemouth were in the lower leagues for years before becoming one of the best outfits in the Premier League. United's recent sides might not have achieved at the level those old stars were used to, but that doesn't mean the players aren't trying. Doubtless, one day the good times will be back again, but the pressure that former players are putting on the United teams of today can only delay the moment that day comes.

Few could deny there are pundits out there who've made a name for themselves by ripping into those who've followed in their footsteps. It's become their schtick. They thrive off it. A year out of the game allowed me to properly pursue my own TV punditry journey. From the start, I was determined to be different. No way would I slate for the sake of it. Rather than being a superstar of the past who, it seems, never made a mistake in their entire career, my punditry would come from the point of view of the vast majority of footballers. I wasn't a world-beater, I wasn't among the very best in the Premier League. I was an average player who was consistent for 10 years. I turned up and did what I needed to do to be effective. For me to appear on TV criticising a player, saying he's had a nightmare, when I've had so many myself would be the ultimate hypocrisy. I had so many games where I wasn't the best, so many games where I got dragged at half-time because I was terrible.

That doesn't mean I won't say what I think. I'll point out if someone's in the wrong position, or hasn't tracked back when they should, because they'll know themselves that they've made a mistake. But I'll also be objective. I'm not going to say someone's a shit player, doesn't deserve to be at a certain club, doesn't deserve to wear the shirt, blah, blah, blah. I won't slag someone off for having a bad game, because that can happen to anybody. It doesn't mean they're a bad player. They don't deserve to be scorned on national television. I just don't feel that's right. Any player, no matter who they are, can go through a run of bad form. And players signed by the top clubs usually are good enough, so maybe, rather than slagging them off, it would be better to look at other reasons why they're not at their best. Maybe they've come to the Prem from another league where the tempo's a bit slower and they're struggling to adapt. Or they've come into an unfamiliar system. Instead of blindly criticising, look a bit deeper into the reason for their performance and chances are you'll find something.

This ability to see the game through the eyes of most footballers, rather than simply get frustrated that they're not beating the opposition out of sight, is one of the biggest pluspoints of having a voice like mine on TV. I'm somebody with a realistic view, rather than an ex-pro who only knows how to barrack and berate. Instead of seeing the game through a cloud of red mist, I can explain clearly what's actually going on. 'This is how the player is thinking. This is what they're trying to do.'

One thing I can guarantee is that, despite what some people might think, no-one on a football pitch is ever trying to underperform. Look at the real world. Who starts a new job and does it brilliantly from day one? And yet there's this expectation that a footballer just walks through the door and delivers pure 24-carat gold. That's not realistic. There's going to be nerves, and, more likely than not, pressure of expectation. The prices clubs are paying for players are getting ridiculous and everyone – fans, owners, managers – is demanding instant results. That's plenty to send anyone off course, without all the chatter from those who, in some cases, should know better. In today's Premier League, the idea of acclimatising to a club has gone. Look at Florian Wirtz after he joined Liverpool from Bayer Leverkusen for £116.5 million. Because he cost so much, there were pundits who couldn't wait to put the boot in. He was being branded a failure after five games. Absolutely crazy.

Equally worrying is the effect those same pundits have on crowds. If all fans hear is how terrible a player is, and among those saying so is a pundit they respect, then it's obvious that some of them will take on that negativity. Suddenly, half the people in the stadium are going round saying that player isn't good enough. Worse, they're directing that negativity towards the player concerned. That's dangerous. All they know of that player is the person they see on the pitch. They don't know what instructions the manager has given them. They hear a pundit slagging them off but for all they know they're doing exactly what they've been told. Obviously, pundits are ex-players so they know to a certain degree what football is about, but they don't know what a manager wants from every player on the field. They're not in the changing room.

Their 'wrong' might be the manager's 'right'. They need to bear that in mind when they sit there judging.

We all have our opinions – football is a game of opinions – and obviously I'm a pundit myself, but I'm also aware there are two sides to every story. None of us in the studio know precisely what's going on in the dressing room. We know that if a player is constantly trying to dribble past someone but keeps losing the ball, or if someone runs offside all the time, then that's wrong. But when it comes to actual shape, or how a team is setting up for a free-kick, or if a team is playing a high line, we haven't a clue what the manager's orders are. What looks a clear case of a player making a mistake might not be that at all. Pundits control the narrative, but that doesn't necessarily mean they're correct. They might even come out with something critical or controversial just so they've got something to say.

Other pundits, thankfully, are more constructive, focusing on how a player can improve rather than what they've supposedly done wrong. What never changes is that, as a footballer, you're under the microscope week in, week out. Take it to heart and even the most mainstream of shows can affect your confidence. Look at *Match of the Day*. While they'll highlight an individual player for doing well, they'll also pinpoint those who've had an off day. They'll show the wayward passes, the misses in front of goal. And that's not easy if you're that player. Some players watch themselves on *Match of the Day* all the time. I only did it when I scored! To be fair, it comes on too late for me anyway. I'm an early bird. I like to get my sleep. I probably should say as well that if you play for West Ham, you're pretty much always last game on. I'm not staying up half the night!

Seventy per cent of footballers love watching football. The other 30 per cent would rather do anything else. Football dominates their life and so when they go home they want to put on a box set or go on the PlayStation. I'm a box set man. Again, it goes back to that thing of never really being a football fan when I was growing up. I used to get jealous watching football on TV – if I was doing that it meant there was no-one for me to play with! Only when I was starting out as a pro did I watch a bit more, because I realised I could learn from studying the best players. At that point of my career, I also listened to pundits more, but as someone who had to fight every step of the way to prove myself as a pro-footballer, I was never going to let what any of them said affect me. I never go out of my way to hear what somebody's said about me. I've been playing the game long enough to know if I've had a poor game. Also, I have a manager. I know for sure he's going to point out any errors and tell me what I need to do to put them right. Managers matter to me, not pundits. They're the ones who put me on the field. They're the ones whose philosophy I'm trying to follow. Pundits can say what they want but they're never going to decide whether I'm on the team sheet. Only one person has that power.

I should point out that there are pundits I respect. I've always loved watching Ian Wright and Micah Richards because not only do they know their stuff but they're such big personalities. Gary Neville and Jamie Carragher, meanwhile, have been around for years but work well together because they've got such great chemistry. Put them in the same studio and there's an abrasiveness about them, a love/hate relationship rooted in the rivalry between their clubs. Coming from Liverpool and Manchester United, they want to get one over each other. Footballers are always going to have that competitive side even when they've retired.

Carragher and Neville were also pioneers of proper in-depth analysis. Over time I've realised there's an art to punditry. Looking back now, I can see I was winging it a bit when I started. It was a case of watch and speak. I can do that. I've been a professional for long enough to be able to dissect what's happening in a game and keep it in my head. But now I write a lot of points down. I think about the key elements of the game, the formations the managers have gone for, and what they're trying to achieve. I make notes about individual players and their performance. I think about the questions I want to ask when the interviews happen at the end of the match. Doing that has made me so much more natural. I feel confident, because I know I'm never going to be stuck for something to say. It's helped me grow into the role.

I've also found I enjoy being live in a ground more than being studio-based. I get a buzz from the rawness of the situation, from hearing the fans shouting, getting a feeling for how they're seeing the game, whereas in the studio you're more reliant on creating that energy yourself. You also only see what the camera's showing you, whereas I prefer to watch the game as a whole, players' movement off the ball, the runs they're making, the more subtle tactical element of what they're trying to achieve.

My aim is not just to be a pundit, but to be a presenter, and that's not easy. It's up to you to drive the conversation, keep it focused, lively, interesting, even when it's a dull 0–0 and there's nothing really to speak about. You might have to do that for four or five minutes. I've had a few practice sessions and you'd be surprised how long four minutes is when you're just talking. Ask a question, someone gives you a short answer and it's straight back to you to carry on the conversation. This is live TV. You can't be stood there umming and ahhing. The first time I tried I was OK for three minutes – talking, asking questions, talking – and then there was a big shout in my earpiece. 'Forty seconds left!' *Shit, I'm running out of things to say!* Luckily, the person I was talking to gave a couple of longer answers and I made it to the end. Otherwise, there would have been 10 seconds of quiet! I'm sure a few boys I've shared a changing room with would be surprised I could ever be lost for words, but the pressure of holding it together when you're live on camera isn't to be underestimated.

Fortunately, as a footballer I've had the best part of two decades reacting in the moment, and that's the best preparation for life as a pundit you could ever have. You really do need to be able to think on your feet. The 2025 Europa Conference League Final between Chelsea and Real Betis in Poland is the perfect example. At one stage I was thrown in at the deep end, answering questions from the studio back in London live down the camera. Those questions came through my earpiece, which would have been OK had there not been a whole load of other chatter going on in the background.

This was live TV. I had to answer. I couldn't stand there look-ing confused and say, 'Sorry I didn't quite catch that.' Each question I heard less and less of. By the time the last one came, I literally just got the first two words. Everything else was drowned out by someone talking, and not even about football. It was something about food. *Oh my God! This is unbelievable!* I took a chance and answered the question I thought I'd been asked. Somehow it worked. I was flying by the seat of my pants, but that's live TV, and I love it, and it's what I want to do. Like football, the unpredictability is part of the buzz.

Luckily, working with TNT I get to see the best in action, ultimate pros like Laura Woods, Jules Breach and Becky Ives who somehow make it all look so easy. They're so chatty and make everybody feel so comfortable, always happy to give me little tips and pointers as I make my own way in TV. It's a steep learning curve. Look at Gary Lineker. He didn't just turn up on his first day and immediately be brilliant. It takes a lot of hard work to get to that point of being so natural, and just like my football, I'm determined to do those hard yards so I can be up there alongside the best in the business.

Steep learning curve it might be, but there's two things I know for sure already. The first is that I'll always be fair about those following in my footballing footsteps. The second is that I'll never compromise on my personality.

FIFTEEN
THE ULTIMATE BUZZ

I'm sat at home thinking about my goal celebrations.
I'm in the Prem now. I really need to up the ante. On
TV, I see The Simpsons. *At that exact moment,*
Homer's lying flat on the ground spinning around in
circles with his legs in a running motion. It's one of
the funniest things I've ever seen. My mind starts
whirring at a similar speed.

On Monday morning at training, I tell the boys
what I'm thinking. 'We've got Sunderland at home
on Saturday. If I score, I'm going to unveil my
"Homer Simpson".' They're all, 'Mikey, no way. You
won't do that!' 'Of course I will!' I tell them. But I
can see they don't believe me.

The day comes. I cut in from the touchline and
thread the ball into the corner of the net. It's a great
goal – to the extent it comes as a bit of a shock!
Shock or not, this is it. I run across the pitch and

*BOOM! drop to the floor. There are 62,500 people
in the stadium watching as I spin around on the turf.
Millions more will see me later on* Match of the Day.
*How many of them have the faintest idea what I'm
doing, I have no idea. Frankly, I don't care. It's a
great celebration and I'm loving doing it. And then in
the back of my mind, a nagging thought appears.
What happens next time I score? How the hell do I
follow this?*

It's a question I get asked all the time – what does it feel like
to score a goal? A lot of players can't answer that, because in
the moment everything becomes a blur, but I always say scoring a goal is full-stop the greatest feeling in the world. People
nod. And then comes the look of puzzlement. 'The best feeling in the world? Surely that's …' Instinctively, their mind has
turned to something completely different, something that
would be very hard to do on a football pitch in front of
62,500 people on a Saturday afternoon.

I try to explain that while sex and scoring goals do have
certain things in common – for instance, neither happens
quite as often as you like! – sticking the ball in the net takes
a footballer to an entirely different planet. It's hands down
one of the best moments of your life, a rush of elation that
consumes you so completely it's almost as if the Earth stands
still. In my case, it's like I'm having an out-of-body experience. While there's nothing louder in a football stadium than
the explosion of emotion that accompanies a goal, to me that
sound is muffled. I know it's happening, because I've been

there so many times, but it's not ringing through me in the same way it does for you as a fan in the crowd.

So stark is the experience that for the first couple of seconds I don't honestly know what to do with myself. That's not the same for everyone. Thierry Henry and Alan Shearer, for example, excelled at keeping a cool head, a composure which no doubt helped them score so many goals in the first place. Me? I'm a different kind of character. I'm totally swept up in the moment. It's my utopia. A place where everything is perfect. Scoring a goal never fails to take me there. It's my fuel. What I thrive on. What keeps me going. I love it every single time. Even when I was playing non-league at Tooting & Mitcham, I was getting a rush from scoring. It's as important to my existence as the blood in my veins. I'm an addict. Constantly chasing that high. But it's a high that can only last a certain length of time. I've got about 30 seconds – 30 unbelievable seconds – before I need to refocus on the game. *Right, OK, let's get back to business!* That business, of course, is chasing that exact same feeling all over again.

That's why, when a goal comes, I'm never going to let it pass with a quick hug of a teammate as I trot back to the halfway line. One thing about the Jamaican culture is that we like to dance, we like to be outlandish, we like to enjoy life in any way possible. Look at Usain Bolt, he was a brilliant athlete, but he was also a party boy. I'm the same. I need no excuse to show the more extravagant side of my personality. My goals were always going to be marked in style. I always wanted to be flamboyant. It's a natural extension of who I am.

Take a look at the video of the little dance that came out when I scored at Wembley for Southampton in the Johnstone's Paint Trophy Final in 2010. Back then very few players seemed to be properly rejoicing in scoring a goal. That was weird to me. After all, goals are the most pivotal part of the game. As a kid, I loved the way Ian Wright, who also played for Tooting & Mitcham, celebrated his goals in a big way, much more than any other player around. On one infamous occasion after scoring for West Ham, not long after Paulo Di Canio infamously shoved referee Paul Alcock to the ground during a game between Sheffield Wednesday and Arsenal, Wrighty ran to the side of the pitch and stood stock still while Neil 'Razor' Ruddock pushed him to the floor. Wrighty then got up and feigned giving Razor a red card. Even for Wrighty that was quite elaborate! More often he'd simply hare around the pitch with his shirt pulled over his head. But, however he chose to celebrate, one thing was clear – for Ian Wright scoring a goal was a massive deal. That's why I loved him, because as well as being a great footballer, he always tried to enjoy himself. Wrighty's attitude was exactly what I wanted to take away from my career. I'm a professional footballer. That's my job. But it's a job I've always thrown myself into.

I also want my kids to see me loving my football, to understand that enjoying what you do in life is important. All too often the fun side of football is forgotten, especially when you become a professional. With all the negativity that surrounds the sport, it's easy to forget why you wanted to play in the first place. BECAUSE YOU ADORE THE GAME! No-one goes into football as a job. You do it because it's a great way to earn a living while doing something you absolutely love. To me, there's always been more to being a footballer than just kicking a ball. It's a celebration of who you are. That's why, from early on, my vision was clear. *When I finish football, I want to be remembered for something more than just my playing career.* I was thinking about it for quite a while, and then it came to me. *Well, Mikey, you've got a few moves in the locker, let's try some of them out.* But then I didn't want to do just anything. If I was going to reel off a move in a Premier League match, it had to be something suitably legendary. I would watch TV and movies for inspiration, and that's how I came up with my very first proper celebration. I mean, if you're going to kick it off somewhere, Homer Simpson is a pretty good place to start. It's probably one of the most iconic things I've ever done in my career, although afterwards Slaven Bilić was quick to dispel any comparisons between myself and the iconic cartoon character. 'They have nothing in common,' he told the assembled press. 'There is no connection between the two. Homer is lazy. Michail is a workaholic.'

Maybe I'd created a bit too much work for myself in this case. I mean, how do you follow that up? If I was going to start celebrating after every goal, maybe I should have done something a little more standard to start with. Even so, I could tell I was on to something. The fans loved the Homer dance and that was all the encouragement I needed. *OK, I'm going to keep doing it.* Although my next attempt was rudely interrupted. This was the game when West Ham finally said goodbye to Upton Park. When I headed our equaliser to make it 2–2 against Manchester United, I'd got about half a second into my pre-planned dance when I was grabbed by Andy Carroll. It was a lesson I learned quickly. In football, you have to get your celebration in early before you're swamped and your moves are lost beneath a tangle of bodies. A few months after that Boleyn Ground farewell, I wasn't going to let scoring in West Ham's first-ever game at the London Stadium go the same way. After heading a late winner, I just about managed to free myself from a mob of teammates long enough to break out the 'Macarena'.

As the goals started to go in, I soon found that the hardest part of my new plan was constantly having to think up new routines. Not just that but making sure they were performed to the absolute best of my ability. In fact, so intent was I on getting my celebrations right that it wasn't uncommon for me to practise them the night before a game. While I didn't rehearse Homer Simpson, no way was I going to take the same risk when I decided to do the 'Worm' (lying flat on my stomach with a rippling motion going through my body) in the hope of unveiling it at the following day's game against Watford. I was in my hotel room for a good while banging that one out. I had to. Get it wrong and I'd never have heard the end of it. The boys would have absolutely slated me. Same went for the 'Running Man' (sliding steps imitating a stationary runner) which I pulled out when I gave the Hammers a 2–1 lead against Liverpool at Anfield. I liked that one so much I dusted it off a couple more times in my career.

If you're gonna do it, you've got to do it right, which is exactly the attitude I took when I unveiled the 'Dan Rue', named after the American whose crazy dance videos have made him a star on Instagram, after scoring the first goal by an opposition player at the Tottenham Hotspur Stadium in 2019. Again, I'd practised the move, busting it out in a couple of clubs, and was pretty happy with the result. Although the combination of leaping and thrusting with my hands held low in front of my hips did raise questions as to what exactly I was doing! For the record, it was more horse-riding than anything else, not a million miles from the 'Gangnam Style' dance I had revealed after finding the net, again versus Liverpool, a couple of months earlier.

Rarely, if ever, were my celebrations spur of the moment. Take the carpet-stroking at the London Stadium. I get that it does kind of look like I've just ended up lying on the floor after scoring against Leicester City, but in fact from the minute West Ham had claret carpet fitted around the pitch, I had my eye on it. In fact, I told the boys that, if I scored, because the club was so buzzing about the carpet's arrival, I was going to get down and give it a stroke. Sounds mad considering the effort I put into some of my other celebrations, but the carpet-stroking became one of my most memorable moments. It's my face that really got people. A kind of dreamy, faraway expression. I look so much like I've found my happy place. For a while afterwards people were saying to me, 'You looked so pleased when you were doing that.' 'What can I say?' I'd reply. 'If there's one thing I really love doing it's stroking carpets!'

However, my all-time best celebration moment, the one that everyone still talks about, came when I broke Paolo Di

Canio's West Ham Premier League goalscoring record, again against Leicester, in August 2021. The move actually dated back to lockdown. With no fans allowed in the ground, my plan was to put a full-size cardboard cutout of myself in the seats, so after I scored I could jump into the stand, sit next to it and applaud myself. There was just one slight hitch. If I went through with it, I'd get a red card. Covid restrictions meant there were strict limits where players could go. Leaping into the stand was a pretty obvious violation. It was a shame that the fans, and myself, didn't get to experience that one. I really do think it would have been amazing.

Instead, once lockdown was lifted, I came up with another version. This time I hid the cutout at the side of the pitch by our reserve goalkeeper Darren Randolph. 'Look,' I told him, 'I've got a cardboard cutout of myself there. If I score today, I'm coming straight to you.' He was like, 'Yeah, don't worry, I've got you.' The other boys, however, knew nothing about it, which meant, when the goal came, Angelo Ogbonna, our Italian centre-back, buzzing for me and my achievement, got me in a very firm headlock. While I was touched that Angelo should be so delighted for me, being caught in a wrestling move was a major threat to my plan. Normally, when someone gets you in a headlock you stand still. But I was having none of it. *I'm not stopping here! There's something I need to do!* I powered on across the pitch. When, finally, I pulled the cutout from its hiding place, everybody was surprised. Even the boys on the bench didn't know. But this was merely the first part of the proceedings. My thoughts were clear. *This will be like nothing anybody has ever seen.* And so, lifting my mirror image above my head, I delivered my own special take on the famous end scene from *Dirty Dancing* when Johnny lifts Baby high above his head. All this happened live on Sky's *Monday Night Football* and in front of West Ham's first full home support since the pandemic. Sadly, it was wasted on Gary Neville and Jamie Carragher. When they interviewed me afterwards both claimed they didn't have a clue what I was doing. Or maybe they just didn't want to admit to having watched *Dirty Dancing*!

Fans tuning in that night may have thought my reaction a little bit over the top. But the way I see it, if footballers want to be treated more like humans and less like robots, they do occasionally need to do a bit of work themselves. How many times have you seen that post-match interview where a player trots out the same old answers you've heard a million times before. 'What matters is the three points.' 'On to next week.' 'We're taking one game at a time,' etc, etc. *Yawn, yawn.* Players are media-trained to stop them saying and doing anything the club believes they shouldn't. But that same media training has crushed people's personalities. I've never allowed that to happen to me. And I think other players are also starting to realise it's good to show the public another side of themselves, who they really are. It's the same with social media. More and more you see them willing to share something of their lives outside football.

Pundits have occasionally tried to mimic my celebrations. They haven't got my style, but, in their defence, I've had those practice sessions in my room. They've got to pull it out the bag, off the cuff. Not helped if they're stood in a big coat, as was the case when I joined Gary and Jamie pitch-side at the London Stadium for an interview after West Ham's 3–1 win over Fulham in 2019. I'd celebrated my goal with a dance from *Ali G Indahouse* – the Eastside/Westside rivalry in the film felt right for this particular cross-London clash. I mean, the two Sky boys did their best, but I don't think they'll be troubling the judges on *Strictly* anytime soon.

I did once share that 'out of my comfort zone' feeling. I was playing a game of *Fifa* with Declan Rice. If I lost, the forfeit was to do a challenge of his choice. Which is why a few days later I found myself doing the backstroke behind the goal after scoring against Burnley. It was a pretty decent attempt, even if I say so myself. It must have been because everyone understood what I was doing (at least they claimed they did!).

Video games were at the root of another goal celebration, this time against Crystal Palace. I'd been playing my brother at *Mortal Kombat* – typically competitive between the two of us – and as I watched the character Raiden, the eternal God of Thunder, launch himself into his trademark torpedo dive, I couldn't help thinking it would make a great celebration. And so it was that at Selhurst Park I headed off down the touchline and launched myself horizontally into the air. Of course, in the real world, gravity gets in the way, so the challenge was to land without doing myself an injury. I was pretty happy with the result, although again it sparked a bit of confusion. *Mortal Kombat* goes back to the 1990s so it was before a lot of younger fans' time. Older supporters didn't have a clue for the opposite reason. By the way, Raiden can teleport too – now that really would have given Gary and Jamie something to talk about!

There was many a time I was tempted to take my celebrations to the next level and bring in a backflip. But while I knew I had the agility and power, when it came to being there in the moment, putting my head back and flipping, I also knew my entire body and soul would be telling me, *Don't do it!* Get it wrong and it's very easy to make a complete arse of yourself. Fail to land that flip and you're across social media for all the wrong reasons. That's without the potential for tendon and ankle damage. I think I did the right thing keeping my feet on the ground. The other thing I've avoided at all costs is hurling myself into the crowd. You never know what might happen. Fingers can find their way into very odd places.

Other times I've planned a celebration and then, in the moment, as the rush has taken hold of me, completely forgotten all about it. I've got my move ready – *I'm going to do this, I'm going to do that* – only to find myself stood in front of the fans thinking, *Oh no, hang on a minute, I forgot!* So, for every Michail Antonio goal celebration people have seen there's definitely a few left in the locker. Sometimes, however, I've pulled it round with the emergency back-up move, 'The Carlton', named after Carlton Banks from *The Fresh Prince of Bel Air*, made famous by the actor Alfonso Ribeiro. Nice and easy, no stress.

The only time I wouldn't celebrate was when I scored against a previous club. It's about showing that little bit of respect, something I learned from the older pros as I was setting out in the game. It's not easy though. Restraining yourself means you're missing out on an unbelievable moment. I scored for West Ham against Forest and didn't celebrate, which meant there was no rush, no buzz, nothing. Again it's like having sex, only on this occasion, just as you get to the best bit, sitting up and saying, 'OK, let's leave it there.' That's exactly what you're denying yourself when you don't celebrate a goal.

VAR is the ultimate passion killer. When it was introduced in 2019, I made the conscious decision only to celebrate a goal to the full if I knew for sure it wouldn't be ruled out (taxi for Richarlison!). Be sure you really have chalked one up before you peel off the latest dance in your repertoire – not an easy judgement, mind you, since video referees have a habit of winding the tape back to an infringement that happened 30 seconds previously. I didn't want to be down on the floor doing the 'Worm' if that happened. How embarrassing would that be? That's the worst thing about VAR, the world's missing my celebrations!

Believe me, it's not been easy to rein myself in. I mean, there are buzzes from goals, and there are BUZZES FROM GOALS! Scoring in the 20th minute is one thing. Scoring in the last minute to win a game, that's something else altogether. Totally outrageous. If I scored a winner in the final seconds against a team I used to play for, I don't know if I could trust myself not to celebrate. I'd apologise later, but I really do think I'd have to lose my mind.

You have to enjoy these moments – because there'll be plenty of other times when things go horribly wrong. Missing a sitter is the worst feeling ever. You know you're going to get crucified for it. It'll be played on TV again and again and again. A single mistake, the same as can be made in any job, except in your case it will be mocked by the multitudes watching it on TV and social media. You can't dwell on those moments. Well, not during the game at least. It's afterwards that it starts to gnaw away at your brain. If you win anyway, not so much, but lose the game, or draw when you should have won, and you are in for a very bad night. It's not just you that you're thinking about; it's the rest of the boys in the team. They're affected by the result too.

Of course, players on other parts of the pitch can make a mistake and a lot of the time pretty much get away with it. Nobody bats an eyelid. It just happens that those made by strikers and goalkeepers are the ones which prove most costly. We're the ones who can change the course of a game. I've literally had nightmares about a bad miss, playing it over and over in my head as I fall asleep, only for it to loom up out of the darkness in the middle of the night. Lying there in a sweat, you're desperate for the next game to come round so you can make it better. Even the next training session, so at least you've got a distraction, something else to focus on. Thankfully, the memory of the howler does disappear – just in time for the next one to come along!

Missing a goal, especially in a big match, is like being punched in the heart. There's times when I'm having bad games and I'll start thinking, *Maybe I'm not good enough. Maybe I'm not who I think I am.* The trick is to bring yourself back to who and what you believe yourself to be. I might miss once, twice, but if on the third attempt I score, then instantly my belief is restored. *Yeah, I can do this!* It's not about being perfect, because no-one's perfect, it's about being the best I can be. Even the very best footballers make mistakes. The team that wins the Premier League will lose a few times along the way. So it's not a crime if I make an error, because I can always make amends. You need that mindset to get to the top. You have to remember that if you make a mistake, there's nothing to stop you doing the right thing next time. Don't let an error live rent free in your head. Do that and you're not focusing on putting it right. When you're playing football, live in the present, not the past. Think about the run you're going to make, the cross you're going to get on the end of. Do that and you also don't need to think about your future – being focused means success will come.

When playing up front, what you really want is to be the penalty taker, a great way to add a few easy (well, that's the idea) goals, and accompanying celebrations, to your tally. Unfortunately, I only ever took three penalties for West Ham, scoring two and missing one, against Newcastle keeper Freddie Woodman at St James' Park. I still can't believe that balls-up even now. I practised for hours the day before, shooting to my left again and again and again (I was going to say that by the end I could have scored blindfold, except I did once take part in a blindfold penalty competition and for the first couple of attempts ended up swinging at thin air!). And then, out of nowhere, Xavi Valero, the West Ham goalkeeping coach at the time, had a word in my ear. 'That's the way their goalie has been diving in the last few games.' It went against my instincts but Xavi's words got in my head, a nagging doubt only added to when Magpies striker and, later, my podcast co-host, Callum Wilson started giving me a bit of a chirp. As I placed the ball on the spot, he was right there. 'You're going left, aren't you? The keeper knows you're going left. That's exactly what he wants you to do. You're going to miss.' I told him to get lost, or words to that effect, but it didn't stop him. Chirp, chirp, chirp. It was like having a sparrow sat on my shoulder.

No prizes for guessing what happened next. I changed my mind and aimed right. And of course that's the way Woodman dived. *Agghh!* I was so upset. Totally devastated. Why didn't I just do what I'd practised? Worse was to follow. David Moyes took me off penalties. I was fuming with myself. I'd worked so hard to get that role, constantly on at the gaffer, 'I want to take pens! I want to take pens!' Initially, he was 'No, no, no.' But I wore him down, and now, because I'd listened to someone else, the opportunity was gone. That was it. There was no going back from there.

Naturally, when, a couple of years later, we got behind the mic, Callum couldn't wait to mention that Newcastle pen. 'I got in his head! That's why he missed. It was me!' Funny guy! But we were always cool with each other, both as players and broadcasters. That's the thing with football. Because we all play against one another so much, there's rarely any real beef between players. Well, unless someone comes across as totally arrogant, in which case you might want to give them a wide berth. But, generally speaking, if I see a footballer out and about, I'll always go over and shake their hand. And the same happens to me. Someone will tap me on the shoulder. 'All right? How's it going?' It's just that, right there, in the heat of the battle, being pally wasn't quite what Callum had in mind. That's how Callum is. Some players are like that, trying to get under your skin all the time, hoping to get in your head and put you off your stride. I've never been one of them. I prefer to keep myself to myself and concentrate on doing what I need to do.

A penalty is such a massive goalscoring opportunity, especially at the top level where chances are hard to come by, that players will do pretty much anything to get the ref to point to the spot. My guess is that footballers have dived for pretty much as long as the game has existed, and yet these days commentators talk about simulation like you've committed murder. Forget a yellow card, you should be serving prison time. That's not to say I don't have a problem with simulation. I do. That problem being that I'm terrible at it. I'm too big to make it look realistic. The little whippy guys are the best – speed into the area, brush another player's leg, and down they go. Me? I'm in slow motion even before they show the replay. I'm hitting that turf like a big old tree cut down after 300 years. With similar sound effects. But I'll still do it! The slightest little touch and I'm hitting the turf.

I don't care what anyone says, as a pro it's what you have to do. Refs are so loath to give pens that you need to give them all the encouragement you can. Maybe if doing the opposite was rewarded a bit more, you'd be more inclined to stay on your feet. But there's so many times where I've tried to stay up after a foul and got nothing. So I'm like, *OK, I'm going down, and if I get a yellow, I get a yellow.* That's happened, not often, but I have been booked. And it's worth it. Every single time, it's worth it. Because if playing for a penalty comes off, it's a massive advantage for your team. Spot kicks are like gold dust. Every striker, every team, is desperate for them. When simulation works for me and I win the pen, I'm not going to apologise for that. Like every other professional, I'm playing for high stakes – my family, my career – and so it's all part of the sport. Call it gamesmanship, call it what you want, but as a professional footballer you get away with as much as you can. We're no different to anyone else. Cricketers don't walk when they've hit the ball and been caught. Athletes shove each other for the best position on the track. In the pursuit of victory, we will push every rule to the limit.

Actually, when you think about it, because everyone does it, no-one ever really gains an advantage. We all cancel each other out. Take Mark Noble, one of the best at winning free-kicks I ever saw. He just knew how to do it. He'd get the ball at his feet, wait for the tiniest contact in his back and go down like a sack of shit. Nine times out of ten the ref would give the foul. Genius at it, he was. And then there was me, who couldn't buy a foul. I once jumped for a ball with Manchester United and England defender Harry Maguire. As we went up, Harry put his arms under my armpits like a forklift truck and literally just hurled me to one side as if I was a child. That's not easy – I'm a heavy guy, more than 90 kg – and it takes a bit of effort. What did the referee decide? 'Play on!' From my position on the ground, I couldn't believe what I was hearing. 'What the actual …?' I pulled a lump of mud from my mouth. But the official couldn't have cared less. 'Carry on!' Unbelievable. And there was Nobes, the slightest tap and the referee was all over him. I was in awe of that bloke, I really was.

Even worse, that Maguire incident happened in the penalty area. But the wrestling that goes on in the box now is so insane that players get away with stuff that, anywhere else on the pitch, would mean an immediate free-kick. Referees won't give those fouls because there'd end up being 10 penalties per half. They don't want to be accused of ruining the game. I don't quite know how it happened, but it's like football's acquired this lawless zone where anything goes. Something will have to be done about it in the end, because it's absolute madness. The only thing not happening in the penalty area is football.

'Live with it!' That's what you end up hearing all the time as a striker, so much so that 'living with it' becomes your default position, although it took me a while to get there. When I started playing up front, I hated it. I just couldn't believe what I was expected to put up with. As a winger I was used to receiving the ball in space, facing my man. Now, with my back to the play, I had centre-halves constantly trying to steamroller me. It felt like there was always a defender right on me, pushing, shoving, getting away with murder. And the referee never seemed to give anything against them. It was like he was watching a different game. That is if he was watching the game at all. I mean, if it's a violation of the rules, surely that's the end of it? Apparently not.

Sometimes it feels like refs and me have rarely got on. If I'm honest, there was an occasion when, if the consequence wasn't a lifetime ban, I'd have punched the official square in the face. West Ham were playing in the quarter-final of the Europa League against Bundesliga champions Bayer Leverkusen. Before the game, most pundits had written us off. Understandably so. We were 2–0 down from the away leg and Leverkusen hadn't lost for 44 games. But on the night, we were brilliant. I headed home after 13 minutes and we were way the better side the whole game. Absolutely cruising. Trouble was the referee, José María Sánchez Martínez, gave us nothing. Me especially. All game, the Leverkusen players were fouling me, tugging at me, bringing me down. It felt like everybody in the stadium could see what was happening except the guy who needed to. I was pushed in the back at one point and was so frustrated with the lack of support from Martínez that I physically punched the ground while staring him right in the face. I hope he got the message. 'If I could swap this piece of turf for you, I would.' When Leverkusen equalised in the last minute, I let my frustration show in the post-match interview. 'I didn't get a decision all game,' I fumed. 'It didn't feel like we were playing against 11 men but 14, including the two linos.' Obviously, as a player you're not meant to criticise the officials, but in that moment UEFA could have thrown the book at me and I wouldn't have cared. I genuinely felt we'd been robbed of a fair result and I was going to have my say.

On the international stage, referees can be equally frustrating. When Jamaica played Ecuador in a Copa América group game in Las Vegas in the summer of 2024, the Chilean referee seemed to go out of his way to give us nothing and them everything. Our captain, Bobby Reid, was losing his head big-time. At one point the ref ignored a clear handball in the area that would have meant a penalty for us. In doing so, he overruled the recommendation of VAR. Never in the world was it the right decision, made worse by a couple of our boys overhearing him tell a couple of the Ecuador players, fellow Spanish speakers, 'Don't worry, I'm giving you the decision.' Bobby, naturally, was raging. At one point he actually ran up to the ref, right in his face. *Shit!* I thought, *He's going to punch him!* I bolted across. 'Bobby! Are you all right?' He wasn't all right. 'He's a cheater!' he kept saying, 'a f***ing cheater!' I tried to pull him away. 'Hey, that's a lifetime ban mate! Come on, just leave it!' We lost the game but at least Bobby stayed on the pitch. Sadly, the refs that Jamaica got in games against Spanish-speaking South American nations often appeared biased. While Bobby might momentarily have had other ideas of how to deal with the situation, all we could do was – you guessed it – live with it.

Referees are so protected. I honestly believe, like players and managers, they should have to go in front of the media and explain themselves. They're a huge part of what happens on the pitch and yet never have to face the music. At the same time, I accept they've got a difficult job. No matter what they decide in a game they're going to be on the end of hate from players and managers on all sides. Keeping both teams happy is an impossible job. And, like all of us, they're going to make mistakes. Even with the risk of bad errors going against me and my team, I'd much rather refs ran the game than VAR. All technology has done is ruin the game. The FA promised VAR would rid the sport of serious human error, but all it's achieved is a load more mistakes being made elsewhere. At the end of the day, VAR still comes down to a person's opinion. Since that's the case, why not just let that person be the referee? At least when the ref makes a mistake you can understand why – things happen quickly, they might not have the best view, etc. But people watching a sequence of play over and over again on video? What's their excuse? It makes the 'experts' at Stockley Park look like fools. Go back to how it used to be and let the game flow naturally. I'm not alone in that view. Pretty much every footballer I know thinks the same. The ones who don't are usually defenders, because VAR is often used to rule out goals.

One last thing. Assists. Let's put this to bed once and for all. An assist is nothing like getting a goal. I used to buzz off it a bit as a winger, but in professional football you soon realise that it's goals that make the money. You need to get the goals. And when you get them, celebrate! With every fibre of your soul, celebrate! You have to, because one day, without you knowing, it will be the last time it happens. And then it's all down to memories. I have the best bank of memories.

I'll feel that carpet running through my fingers forever!

SIXTEEN
RETIREMENT

I'm with Clark Carlisle, a high-profile example of a footballer who really struggled in retirement. Clark's played for some big clubs, including QPR, Leeds and Burnley, and was hit with depression during and after his career, making attempts on his life during both those periods.

I meet him at a point where my own career is at a crossroads after the crash. He tells me about the shock of retirement, how institutionalised he'd become as a footballer, and how he felt unable to define himself as a person away from the game.

His words come as a shock. I resolve, whatever happens, not to allow myself to suffer the same fate.

There was one good(ish) thing about being out of the game for more than a year – it gave me a long look at what retirement might be like. A lot of footballers are so invested in the game they don't get even a glimpse of the 'afterlife'. And then the end comes, often without warning, and hits them right between the eyes.

Retirement is a big leap for a footballer. We're detached from real-life in so many ways. While we might have had a couple of part-time jobs as teenagers, most of us have never done a normal day's work in our lives. We're also used to having a lot of stuff done for us. We're told where we need to be and when. The rest of it is sorted by our club. Agents, meanwhile, are there to deal with the financial stuff. If we're lucky we'll have a partner who takes most of the strain on the domestic front. Because we're away so much, inevitably it's down to them to do the majority of the hard work with the kids.

No wonder then that retirement comes as a shock. I've heard it compared to people coming out of the army and back into civvy street. I understand the similarity because, like them, we're institutionalised. There's a definite transition to be made, and some, inevitably, find it easier than others. I've never known anyone be scared of retirement, but time and again I've spoken to ex-footballers who tell me, 'You know what? You don't realise how much you'll miss it 'til it's gone.' Many regret stopping when actually they could have played on. Maybe not at the level they were previously, but they could still have had a few more years pulling the boots on every Saturday, enjoying being part of a team and everything that goes with it. That's the thing: it's not just the playing, it's the banter, the changing room, the sense of purpose that comes from just having somewhere to be every day. I can see why players lose that sense of purpose. For years everything has been about the next challenge, and the next and the next. Suddenly, all that's ahead of them is a void. For a naturally competitive person that's hard, a bigger challenge than any that's come before, and one that, rather than as part of a group, they're faced with alone.

Fans see well-known players go down the divisions later in their careers and think, *Why don't they just give it a rest?* But saying that ignores the basic enjoyment of playing, of just being in and around football. Remember, this was our hobby before it became our job. Yes, there are times when it's stressful and annoying, when the politics of football clubs, or more likely the people within them, leaves you ripping your hair out in frustration. But underneath it all, you're still making a living from your hobby. That's why, even when the crowds and big games are a distant memory, you still get players turning out for the smallest of non-league teams, way down the pyramid. They love football and need it to be part of their life.

Some players cement that long-lasting connection by going into coaching or management. Do that and you're still right there in and around the changing room. You're still getting that 'kick'. Coaching at a club isn't on my radar right now. I'm in the process of completing my UEFA B licence which will allow me to coach kids, something I've always enjoyed, but do I want to go into coaching full-time and be in the pro-football environment for another 20 years? I really don't know if I could do that. Coaching is so demanding, an unforgiving results-based environment, and again you're under the control of a football club, in the eye of the storm. That's not to say I don't think I've got something to offer, but for now I'd rather talk to players on a consultancy basis – go into clubs and speak to strikers and wingers, give them the benefit of the experience I've accrued over the years. There's another thing: opportunities are definitely much harder to come by for Black managers. Compare the number of Black players in the game to the number of Black managers and there's a clear disparity. That's no accident. There has to be a reason somewhere.

I'd never rule out being a manager, but right now I feel like I've already given up enough for football. I've had my kids young and so I've missed a lot of their growing up. I don't want that to be the same when they're older. I'm not going to lie, there were times during my recovery when I enjoyed the freedom of being away from the game. There's so much control in football – you need to be at this place at this time, do this, do that – and training with the Under-21s at West Ham, there were days when I could take it or leave it. For the first time in a long while, I began to see another side of life. Whereas before if one of my kids was in a school play I'd always have to skip it, now I'd be thinking, *You know what, I'm going to be there this time.* Same with having a day off. In football, ring in sick and you still have to go in to be examined by the club doctor. Away from the game I was free to make the decision for myself.

This new-found ability to do what the hell I wanted really hit home when I went on holiday with the kids for half-term. As a player, those kinds of opportunities are gone. I know only too well how football is a thief of family time. I've been playing professionally for 18 years and in 11 of those I've had to leave my family on Christmas Day to go into training. Sometimes that entails travelling and spending the night in a hotel ahead of the game the next day. These days, in the Premier League at least, there aren't many games on Boxing Day. Fans aren't happy with that, but it does give players that opportunity to make those precious memories with their families. Those are our kids' memories as well, remember. A number of times I've had to walk out the house at midday on Christmas Day – that's really tough on a kid. Sometimes they'd barely have got out of bed and I'd be away. I don't want their memories of Christmases with Dad to be of me disappearing out the door.

Of course, when it comes to staying in the game there's only so many coaching jobs to go round, and it's not for everyone anyway, so a lot of lads step away from football with no idea of what they want to do next. They end up sitting around the house feeling like caged animals. Life loses meaning. Whereas once it was unpredictable, fun and exciting, now it's just boring. After a few months of that they become aimless, depressed, lost within themselves. As someone who's always set myself goals, I know I'll never allow myself to end up like that. I want to finish football and walk straight into the next chapter of my life. Even in the depths of my recovery, rarely would you find me just sat in my house. I'd got my business interests to look after, I was exercising, getting fitter, working on TV and constantly talking to people about new opportunities. And then there's my kids. Bored?

Not much chance of that! Keeping busy is something I'll always do. I'll adapt, like I already have done. I've had to change a lot of my traits. Number one being I need to be better on my phone. As a footballer, I'd deal with things in my own time, but real-life doesn't work like that, especially when you're trying to run or start businesses.

I also want to further my international career. I'm one of those footballers who's had the opportunity to play for the country of my heritage and the country of my birth. Some might find that odd, but to me that's exactly how it should be. Growing up, I lived two lives. Inside the house I had this Caribbean culture going on. Mum and Dad both spoke patois. My friends would come over and not be able to understand the broken English they heard. We ate Caribbean food constantly, things like curried goat, and rice and peas, to the point where, when I got to about 10 years old, I couldn't stand it anymore. I couldn't wait to get down to the chip shop to get some chicken and fries! And that was me all over: outside the house I was into very English things. I was totally 50/50, a complete mix of England and Jamaica. I knew everything about both cultures because I was totally immersed in both. Every year, for the six-week school summer holiday, Mum would take me to Jamaica to stay with relatives. Even before I made it as a footballer, I'd seen a lot more of the world than a lot of the kids around me in the classroom. And yet that was my British side, being around my mates at school.

Naturally, I was qualified to play for Jamaica through my parents, but when the call came as I started to impress with

West Ham, initially I turned down the chance. It made sense that I should look towards what I could achieve with the Three Lions. After all, it was a side I was equally invested in. Often at school, if England were playing a match overseas in the daytime, we'd get to watch in a special assembly. Even so, when Sam Allardyce took over from Roy Hodgson, after England had been knocked out by Iceland at Euro 2016, I had no great expectation of being picked. But, at the same time, I knew it was a possibility. After all, a handful of players, Jamie Vardy being the highest profile at that time, had shown me it was doable. In fact, Vardy's journey from non-league to England in just four years was one of my main sources of inspiration. *If he can do it, why can't I?* And then one day, after West Ham lost 2–1 at Manchester City, I was called over by our physio as I walked into the changing room.

'You've been called up!' he told me.

'Yeah, right!' I replied. There's plenty of banter knocking around football and I had no reason to think this wasn't just someone having a little pull of my leg.

'No, seriously!' he replied. I looked at him. *Surely, he's got to be bullshitting, right?* But his face never changed. *Jesus! He's serious!* I couldn't believe it. I was absolutely buzzing. And then the enormity of being selected for my country hit me and I started to feel properly emotional. I actually needed a little bit of time to myself to take it all in – the journey I'd been on, the setbacks, the self-belief I'd had to draw upon every time someone said I didn't have what it takes. And it looked like Allardyce was thinking along the same lines when he mentioned my rise from non-league in his press conference.

'If you've got guts and determination and desire,' he told the assembled media, 'it shows how much it means.' He was right. I deserved my chance as much as anyone else. I'd performed at a high standard in the Premier League, so much so that I'd become impossible for the manager of the national team to ignore. My pace and power had proved a handful at club level. Why couldn't I take that on to the international stage? Big Sam saw me as his kind of footballer: no holds barred, totally committed to the cause. He was famous as a club manager for liking players who were resilient, and I fitted the bill exactly. He also said he liked my athleticism and that I delivered an end product – the ball in the back of the net.

With Allardyce at the helm I looked well set for a good few England caps. There was only one problem – he lasted just 67 days in the post. During his one game in charge, I was an unused substitute as England won 1–0 in Slovakia thanks to a last-gasp winner from my old Southampton teammate Adam Lallana. It was massively frustrating not to get on the field, especially in a game where it needed someone to break the stalemate. In the end, though, Big Sam put attacking options Dele Alli, Theo Walcott and Daniel Sturridge on ahead of me. He did, however, have the decency to tell me why I'd not made it off the subs' bench. 'I wanted to put you on,' he told me, 'but because it was my first game I needed to go with experience.' I respected him doing that, taking the time to explain his thinking, and, while I might have disagreed, I could see where he was coming from.

If Allardyce had picked me, I'd have impressed. I know I would. A hard game, against opposition difficult to break down, was perfect for my 'get the job done' style. I felt hopeful, though, that I'd get another chance. And then, after a newspaper investigation into off-field activities, the next thing I knew he was forced to resign, with Gareth Southgate coming in as a replacement. I got called up under Gareth for a World Cup qualifier against Lithuania but had to withdraw after picking up a hamstring injury. The same injury also ruled me out for a friendly against Germany, which was when, I'm sure, I'd have finally made my England bow. Having picked a young side, Gareth gave practically every sub at least a few minutes' run-out. That was my chance. After that, it never came again. It was as if I wasn't meant to play for England. Like it wasn't my calling. That's how philosophical I was about it. It wasn't meant to be and that was that.

Which meant, ultimately, as I drifted into my thirties, I turned my attention back to Jamaica. Straight away I couldn't have loved it more. Playing in Jamaica is just the best vibe. The stands are absolutely shaking. There's music going on, speakers as big as houses, people dancing. It's like a party with a football game going on in the background. One of my best-ever goals came for Jamaica. Playing against the USA in a World Cup qualifier in 2021, I picked up the ball near the halfway line and cut inside to launch an absolute thunderbolt into the top right-hand corner from almost 30 yards.

More than anything, whatever the future holds, I hope that my mental health journey will always be an inspiration to those finding it difficult to come to terms with life outside of football. Clark Carlisle showed me how, with retirement, all too easily can come a loss of identity. We're all defined by our jobs to some degree but especially so as a footballer. It's not just what we are, it's who we are, to us and everyone else. It's all we ever wanted to do, and then we made it, and so that's what we became. It's not easy to have that slip away from you; to experience that sudden transition from being the centre of attention to being yesterday's man. Overnight, the phone stops ringing, the media attention vanishes. As a footballer, your retirement is a story, what happens next not so much.

The word 'retirement' doesn't exactly help. It's something you think about happening to someone in their sixties, or older. Chances are that person will be looking forward to a long-awaited rest, but for a footballer it can come totally out of the blue. A couple of bad injuries and it could be game over before they're 30. As I know all too well myself, football and sentiment don't mix. When you're gone, you're gone. There's no-one offering you a magic fix. You're out there on your own and that's that. Meanwhile, football carries on without you like nothing has happened, like you were never even there in the first place.

Out of the game, a player might experience a new and unusual kind of pressure. Maybe they'll feel the weight of trying to keep their family enjoying the lifestyle they're used to. Or of trying to maintain a happy face when inside they feel totally down and dreadful. Footballers are used to pressure, but of the sporting kind, and so in this strange and hostile new arena they find escape in dangerous areas: drinking too much, gambling, or whatever. Before you know it, the money has disappeared and a once happy marriage is on the rocks. It happens so often, players pushing a problem further and further down the road, their self-esteem and mental health vanishing into the distance with it. But, sooner or later, you have to deal with this stuff.

Clark, fortunately, turned his life around. Like me, he's a great advocate for therapy. But there are players facing this unknown and often frightening new world all the time. It's vital they know they can access help – and not feel any stigma for doing so. The last thing anyone needs in a situation like this is to feel judged. Thankfully, I know from talking about my problems that the only judgement you receive is, 'Well done – you did the right thing there, mate.' All you get from people, in and out of the game, is respect.

Even so, players aren't used to being afraid. While they take most things in their stride – let's face it, a new challenge comes along every weekend – there's a big difference between the tests that a sporting life throws up and those to be faced in the real world. That's why I'll tell anyone who'll listen that the best thing they can do is have an honest conversation about their problems. Not only am I living, breathing proof of the benefits of doing so, but my own experience tells me there are plenty of amazing people out there more than happy to help, more than happy to put you back on an even keel. All any of us needs to do is talk to them.

SEVENTEEN
THERAPY

I'm in my own world. As if I'm living in the shadow of my body. Everything seems distant. Like I'm looking at the world from the back of my head instead of through my eyes.

I did eventually get to savour the feeling of winning the 2023 Europa Conference League Final. But it was several months until I truly began to process that night in Prague after we beat Fiorentina 2–1 to clinch the trophy. It's the best thing that's happened to me in my football career. It's just that it came at one of the most difficult times of my life.

The period of disaffection in and around football which descended on me in the months before that game meant that for a good while I was just living day to day. I was so lucky that I had Dom, my physio, around – someone who'd notice the changes in my mood. He had that golden ability to see that a person was struggling. Because he did a lot of my rehab work after injuries, we'd spend a lot of time chatting, just me and him. That meant talking about not just football but all sorts of things. Proper chats, really opening up to him. He was an outlet for me at the most vital of times. In fact, it was Dom who first began talking about therapy. It was a real lightbulb moment. 'That's what I need!' Until that point my reaction was like a lot of people's. *Therapy, that's for crazy people, right?* I don't mean any disrespect to anyone who's gone down this route, or the therapists who do such a great job. All I'm saying is, like a lot of people, for a long time that's the view of counselling and therapy I had in my mind. I was, of course, totally wrong.

I know for some people the hardest thing about therapy is actually opening the door and going into the meeting room for the first time. I'll be honest, before I did exactly that towards the end of 2022, I couldn't have ever imagined it would be something I'd do. But at the same time, I've always been the kind of person who'll try anything once. If don't like it, fine, but at least I know I've given it a go. Anyway, by the time I turned that handle I'd come to terms with my need to take the plunge. I'd chatted about how I was feeling to a couple of people close to me and, while they were, of course, trying to help, from my point of view it felt like they were telling me everything would be OK when I knew underneath that things were a lot more complex. I get why they were saying those things, and they were doing their level best, but their approach wasn't what I needed. It didn't reflect what was going on in my head. I had to get what I was feeling off my chest; to express myself and understand what I was going through. I felt lost – and wanted to be found. I wanted to find myself again.

A therapist gets you to understand what you're feeling, whereas friends and family are trying to make you feel better. Like 'It'll be OK. Just remember all the good things you have in your life.' They care and so they want to make it easier for you. But making something easier is different to getting through a deep-seated and mentally challenging situation. It doesn't mean that you're really going to get over anything. That only comes from understanding your emotions, and the depth of the reasons why you're struggling, and it's then that therapy is the route to go down – not so much about *how* you feel as *why* you feel. Suddenly, you're thinking about who you are from a totally different perspective. You're addressing elements of your life you never thought possible, taking apart the pieces and putting them back together in a way that, finally, makes sense. And as you do so, all that trapped emotion, all those feelings, come pouring out.

So there I was, taking a step that had once seemed as distant as walking on the moon. The counsellor looked at me: 'How can I help you?' And that was it. I burst into tears. I live in a very alpha world. Football's not a place where, to any real degree, you're allowed to be emotional. Yet here I was, sobbing proper uncontrollable tears. And it felt like such a relief. I'd been pushing so much down for so long, and now finally all that mental pain could come gushing out. It was like I could breathe properly again. I could feel the walls falling away in my head, fresh air flooding into the space. It was so, so liberating. The most incredible feeling, like the flood-gates of my heart had been unlocked.

When, finally, the tears subsided, I started talking about all the issues still tugging at my insides. Things I thought I was long over, when actually I was so far from that being the reality. I spoke about how I was struggling with my marriage, and also my game. I explained how football had always been my saviour in times of pain, how it had always allowed me to block out trouble, except now it wasn't working. I knew straight away this was what I needed to do. From that point on I started going to sessions weekly. I'd sit and talk and try to get everything off my chest.

However, by the time the Europa Conference League Final came round, the situation with my marriage was affecting me massively. I'd been with Debbie 12 years. We'd been great together, as shown by our beautiful children, only for what we had to fall apart. There was no blocking out that situation. Even the greatest moment of my footballing life couldn't push the negativity away. I aways portrayed myself as very confident, and I genuinely thought I was the happiest person there could be. My entire personality was based on positivity. But now I was swamped with self-doubt. I tried my best to be upbeat. I did a couple of interviews in the stadium after the game and was all about what a great time me and the boys were having. But I was pretending. Truth is, I was gone inside. How else do you explain sleeping on a bus full of footballers buzzing off their minds?

Naturally, I spoke about what happened with my therapist. I wanted to know more about how and why I'd reacted in that way. I thought about other off-the-pitch things and how they'd affected me. When my dad died in 2020, for instance, I played my best football for West Ham. I scored eight goals in a month because I was able to blank it out. *OK, I'm not going to let this affect my football. I'm not going to let it affect how I play. I can deal with it once I've finished the game.*

In Prague, I'd reached again for emotional detachment – the numbness that, therapy has made me realise, is my safety net. I can remove myself from a situation and park it miles away in the distance. There might be brief moments when something will click and there'll be a burst of emotion, but otherwise I'll not actually think about it. Dad's death is the perfect example. My therapist says I've still not dealt with it and one day I should expect it to hit me like a brick wall. I hear what they're saying. I know stamping down your feelings isn't healthy. But I also know, in my profession, it's a blessing as well as a curse.

Footballers perform on a public stage. If we've got something serious going on in our lives, we can't work from home or hide in a corner of the office. We've got to perform, and we want to perform, for our families, our teammates and ourselves. Detachment means footballing freedom. Or, at least I thought it did. The fact that, earlier that same season, I'd found myself stood on a pitch wishing I wasn't there meant that clearly wasn't the case. My head was completely clogged up. At that point, I needed a complete mental reset. For three years I'd played pretty much non-stop. Anything, even playing football, can get repetitive after a while. The thing I loved had become something I never thought it could ever be – a job. Something you go and do every day and then once a month a pay-packet drops into your account. Worse, I'd started disliking football, to the extent that during a particularly bad game a thought went through my head. *I want to get injured.* Crazy, but that was the only way I could see me getting that mental rest I so desperately needed. Not long after, I went away with Jamaica and injured my medial knee ligament in a game against Canada. Ironic really – amid all the negativity I was feeling, playing for Jamaica was the one footballing outlet I was still enjoying. The result was three months out.

As I progressed through therapy, I came to understand a truth I'd never realised: I still deal with bad times the same way I did as a kid. Experiences which happened to me way back then still affect me now – because childhood is when you learn how to deal with problems. You might be an adult, might be able to look after yourself, to protect yourself, but you're still operating on the same emotional framework you did as that kid. That really surprised me. 'I ain't behaving like a child!' 'No,' agreed the therapist, 'you aren't behaving like a child. You've just learned how to deal with things as a child.' As soon as they said it, I saw it. I thought back to my early years. It was exactly the case. Like when I was 14 and the lads who I thought were my friends threw me under the bus in the worst possible way. One day those 'friends' went out and stole a bike. Because they were still in school uniform they were caught in no time. Their response was to say that I'd done it. I'd hung around with these so-called mates for three years. I learned a lesson that day: people weren't to be trusted. They were liable to say one thing and do entirely another. That, and other negative situations, added up to me pushing problems deep down into myself. Never ever dealing with them. The only time I felt confident in myself was when I was playing football. Away from the game, not so much. There were times growing up when I struggled to make friendships. Outside of my brother John I was never really tight with anyone.

Something else the therapist said pretty much stopped me in my tracks. In normal life, the playground behaviour stops. As an adult, you don't generally get people making comments, criticising, spreading rumours. In football, it just carries on. You have to step out on the field with all the criticism and opinions that come with it. Different time. Same shit. Magnified. I couldn't stop thinking about that for hours.

I thought also about the full-on family environment I grew up in. Generally, I was a happy kid. I loved my childhood. It was unbelievable, probably the best days of my life. But because I was so young I didn't really get much opportunity to speak. My house was busy. We had a three-bed terrace but, including family from Jamaica coming to stay, there could be anything from 10 to 13 people living there. And then, every Sunday, all my nieces and nephews would come over. The Antonio family is ridiculously big! At the same time, I was a people-pleaser. If I wanted to do something, but someone had a different idea, my immediate reaction would be, 'OK, let's just do that.' I'd bury my own wishes and just get on with it.

I was constantly suffocating my true feelings, never allowing the real me to exist. Keeping myself busy was my answer. When I wasn't busy, or lacked a target, I hated it. I got bored. I always needed to be doing something. I'd find myself messaging friends. 'Come on, let's get out there – let's go and do something!' Anything except sit at home. A side effect of that was my boundaries could become too low. I was letting people into my life too easily. It all goes back to self-esteem and not building any as a child. My therapist tells me I need to establish my boundaries, let people know how I feel, because all that will happen otherwise is things will get worse. It's better to let people know how you're feeling than to have hurt burning away inside.

It's good to have some sort of explanation for the way you are. On a very basic level, to understand yourself a bit better. But I find it frustrating that things from so long ago could still affect me now. I've learned that quite a few issues have lingered on into adult life. High up on that list is trust. I've faced a lot of problems on my own, because at times the only person I've trusted is me. It's a part of my life, my mentality, I'm hoping to approach in a different way. I know I need to change to a position where I'm dealing with problems like an adult.

That's why I'll carry on doing therapy. My great hope is that other men reading this will take the same journey. A lot of us guys won't look at ourselves in terms of mental health, because for so long the narrative has been that we're not meant to do so. That applies to football as much as anywhere else. For generations of players, looking after your head meant getting out of the way of a high boot, not keeping an eye on what was going on inside it. Had I experienced difficulties towards the start of my career, no way would I have accessed therapy or spoken out. It's not so much that I'd have been scared of being mocked, it's just that the environment was so different. There just wasn't the space in the game to discuss stuff like that. Now I'm older and have experienced more of life, I've reached a stage where I'm comfortable enough with myself to speak about my struggles. And if someone as big (and as loud!) as me can do therapy, then hopefully others will feel comfortable doing the same. I've had several Premier League players ask me about therapy, wanting to know what it's like, how it works, what it's done for me – and what it could do for them and their problems. I've even introduced players to therapists. I love that there are players, the same as I did, taking that first step to a better future – a step away from the cliff edge. Whatever stigma remains about talking openly about mental health seems to be getting less and less every day. I believe that everyone, no matter who they are, what they do, should be encouraged to access therapy. It's such a simple way to bring clarity to your life. Analysing yourself and getting help is always worth it.

Equally, I know there'll be people who'll never get that a footballer could need help with their head. The outside chatter is we've got everything we could ever possibly want. Even today, when people are more educated about mental health than ever, I still see it. Whenever a player opens up about their issues, social media is full of ill-informed people asking, 'How can you be upset? You make thousands of pounds a week and you're upset? You earn loads of money, live in a great house, mix with amazing people, go wherever you want. What could you possibly have to be pissed off or feel bad about?' But that isn't real life. That's just nonsense. Some of the richest individuals in the world have taken their lives. People need to realise that money itself isn't happiness. You can't buy happiness. It has to come from within. To say that money makes you happy ignores the person you are as a whole. It ignores your past. It ignores everything you've been through, good, bad, or indifferent. Just because you've got X amount of money in the bank, what the hell difference does it make? If you believe that happiness comes only from money and possessions, then you'll never know who you really are. You'll never find contentment. You'll be chasing happiness the rest of your life. I think about kids in Africa who haven't even got shoes, but still you see them playing football with a smile.

The same goes for the face you wear. Even when I was going through difficult times I'd go into the changing room and make the boys laugh. History is full of those types of people. Look at the actor and comedian Robin Williams. He seemed like the happiest, funniest, most upbeat guy you could meet. And then the world looked up one day and he was gone. These tragedies happen again and again and yet they never seem to register. Robin Williams had all the money. He had everything he could possibly want in life. And yet the happiness, the security he needed to feel within himself just wasn't there. No-one better proves the point: what you see isn't always what you get.

This is why for so many years I've been saying that footballers aren't robots. It's naïve to believe that we're different from everyone else, that we don't think about our lives, our happiness. Like anyone, we operate at our best when our minds are uncluttered, when we feel free. At that point we almost are robots, because we're operating automatically. Once the outside thoughts start messing up the circuitry, that's when things start going wrong. The mechanism slows down, and it becomes confused in its decision-making. It takes wrong turns. If your mind is tense then your body will be too, and performance inevitably suffers. Of course, the worse you perform the more tense you get, a difficult spiral to escape from, which is why you need to share. A situation like that will never get better by bottling it up.

It's long been one of those classic football questions. Do problems off the pitch affect performance on it? In my experience, while I've known players who can somehow push an off-field problem to one side until the game is over, they're few and far between. More likely, whether they're conscious of it or not, it will hit them negatively. A footballer plays at their best when their mind is clear. Look at my West Ham teammate Lucas Paquetá. Charged with breaching FA betting rules in 2023 after claims he'd deliberately tried to get referees to give him yellow cards as part of a spot-fixing scandal, he was living a nightmare for two years while he was under investigation. He was actually in tears after he was booked against Tottenham during that period. Lucas just couldn't perform like he wanted because the situation was constantly nagging at the back of his mind. When, finally, he was cleared, the mental shackles were off and he was able to go back to playing the kind of football that had attracted the interest of Manchester City before his world fell apart.

Remember, it's not just the playing. As an elite footballer there are people talking about you 24/7. There's no escape from it. 'You need to let your emotions out,' my therapist tells me. 'If you don't, they'll come out in another way.' And that's exactly what we see happening in football. Phil Foden talked about how off-the-pitch matters affected his form in the 2024–25 season, how he'd been left physically and mentally burned out. 'Sometimes there's things in life that are bigger than football,' said the Manchester City and England midfielder, and he was right. Same as there's things in life that are bigger than any job. We all have to put work second and ourselves first sometimes.

There have been some high-profile tragedies in football over the last few years. Matt Beard, the former Liverpool women's boss, and German goalkeeper Robert Enke both took their own lives. When, towards the start of my own career, I heard about Gary Speed, who did the same aged just 42, I felt so upset for him and his family, so sad that he wasn't able to find the happiness within himself. I know also that, because I was only 21, I didn't understand mental health issues like I do now. Therapy has shown me that I was the kind of person who shrugged negative experiences off. My mindset was, 'OK, this is the way life is.' I was happy-go-lucky. I'd smile and forgive, when actually I was hurting inside. So, when Gary Speed died, my attitude was, *How can anyone reach the stage where they want to take their own life?* From the outside, Gary looked like he had everything – the family, the career, the lot. But the outside can be deceptive.

When it comes to emotions, a lot of men divert attention from themselves. They bounce it back where it came from. They might be hurting inside, they might be struggling, but still they want to act like everything is OK. I remember a few years ago being really struck by a video Norwich City put out for World Mental Health Day. It featured two middle-aged fans meeting week after week at Canaries games. One of them is massively upbeat, constantly on his feet shouting and cheering. The other seems permanently down, never excited, going through the motions. And then one week one of them doesn't turn up. It's the 'happy' fan – he's taken his own life. That little film hit home massively with me. I was struggling at the time, and yet there I was laughing, running jokes with everybody. Inside I was a mess, but anyone who saw me would have thought the exact opposite. Even when I'm stressed, I always come across as upbeat, but I've come to see that people who seem the most easy-going types can be desperately unhappy inside.

Fortunately, mental health awareness in football is much more prominent now across the board. Every year the PFA sends counselling experts into clubs to explain why keeping a tag on how we're feeling is so important and what help is available. If I'm honest, though, footballers aren't always keen on this kind of thing. Meetings like this always happen after training when players have one eye on going home, getting off to the gym, or whatever. The last thing they want is to be kept behind. I've been in those sessions, looked around, and wondered if anyone's really listening. But it's important they happen, because maybe in that room there is someone who, unknown to everyone else, is struggling, and who, right there and then, is beginning to realise they need help. A PFA counsellor also exists in total separation from the club. That player can talk to them in the absolute knowledge that none of what they say will be fed back to the management. Clearly there are protocols to follow if someone says they're feeling suicidal, or might harm themselves, but other than that it's vital that players trust a counsellor to keep everything that's said to themselves.

I spoke to a PFA therapist myself for a while. I found him easy to connect with because, as an ex-footballer, he understood everything players go through. Sometimes that's important, especially if an issue is sport-related, and I did pass his details on to other players who I thought might benefit from his help.

Football is part of life, which means it can be a big strain on your emotions. So many peaks and troughs. How do you maintain any kind of mental level in that kind of fevered environment? As a player, the beauty of therapy is that the tools it gives you to deal with real life also help to build more consistent performance. That has to be the way, because you're no longer carrying the same burden on to the field. For instance, therapy has made me trust in my own honesty. I find it so much easier to say no, and don't put myself in situations which are liable to get me down. Similarly, whereas before I internalised my lowness, now I can talk about depressing situations, verbalise them, understand them, come to terms with them, add some context or perspective, and move forward. 'What's any of that got to do with football?' you might ask. But this new-found mental freedom allowed me to rediscover my passion for the game. I found that, as time went on, football itself became less and less of an issue for me and so would form a smaller part of the counselling process. Truth is, my long-term therapist doesn't understand sport at all, but they do get me as a person, which is why I so enjoy speaking to them. It's important to find that one person you really click with, who you really do believe you can trust.

To have clarity about myself is unbelievable, but it's important for me to say that everyone is different. The exact thing that worked for me might not work for somebody else. I can't speak for everyone in terms of what they might need. It's important that they find that help, those answers, themselves. But if anyone asks me about having therapy, I always say it's the best thing they could ever do. I tell them it will change their life. I also tell them it's something they should do whether they feel down or not.

No matter how you're feeling, therapy helps you navigate your way through life, full-stop. It wasn't until I felt lost myself, to the point where I didn't really know who I was anymore, that I began to see how badly your emotions can pull you down. Ignoring the presence of those feelings, letting them carry on and on, is never the right option. While it can be difficult, you need to face up to them. Believe me, it really is so much better, for everyone. If you're feeling positive about yourself, you're easier for everyone else to be around.

One last thing. I genuinely believe we need a therapy revolution in this country. Therapy should be there, free of charge, for everyone, at different stages of life. Imagine if kids could talk openly at the age of 10 or 11, expressing how they're feeling before that giant and often unnerving step up to secondary school. Those same kids should be offered another chance to talk to someone when they're 16, figuring out what they want to do with their lives, and again as young adults aged 21 when the road ahead can feel daunting. From there, I'd offer free counselling at other landmark moments. At 30 perhaps, when life isn't always going the way people might hope, and 45, when middle-age has arrived – another possible flashpoint. Maybe even 60, as potentially you're faced with more difficult life choices. I think we should normalise therapy as much as possible and scheduling it into people's lives is a really positive way of doing so. Were that to happen then hopefully more people would feel like me, like they've hit the refresh button in a way that, in darker times, could never have been imagined. I've recalibrated mentally. I've reached a stage of calmness. I feel OK with life again. I'm accepting of it. This is what it's going to be.

Therapy has allowed me to embrace and understand my emotional side. I can have moments when I'll cry, but I can also live in the present and have gratitude for everything I have – my family, my children and all I've achieved. I sometimes struggle, like we all do, but I also know what's good in my life.

The old Michail has come back.

EPILOGUE

I don't get flashbacks. I've driven down that same road in Essex again, no problem. I've even tried to work out where I crashed, but having no memory of the accident means it's impossible. There have been times when I've actually said to myself, 'I wish I *could* remember.' But then I'll think, *I'm happy I don't*, because it would only bring mental distress. I'm glad of the blank. I can get into my car now (I'm going to stay away from sportscars from now on), be comfortable and not have any fears. Had I consciously lived those moments it would have been a whole different story. I feel like there'd be a fear, a phobia even, of all kinds of things – rainy days, trees, being in a car, whatever.

What I do know is that everything happens for a reason. That's not easy to say about a car crash which nearly killed me, but I do think that's the case. A long period of recovery allowed me to assess life as a footballer in a way that would never otherwise have happened. While therapy was already a big part of my life when I hit that tree, I hadn't ever thought of sitting down and peeling back the layers on a life at the epicentre of my sport and its many and varied ups and downs. For most people, football is something that dips in and out of their lives – a Saturday afternoon perhaps, or a Tuesday night. But what if it's your everyday, your 24/7? What if it's your oxygen? And, what if, without you even noticing, it becomes your poison?

That's why I wanted to write this book, to throw open the doors on that world. Not in a 'woe is me' way. Anyone who knows me will tell you that's not the person I am. And anyway, being a Premier League footballer is as crazy and amazing an existence as you might imagine. But in a way, that will hopefully act as a reminder that somewhere beneath the madness of the modern game sits a bunch of people pretty much the same as everybody else. Same hopes, same fears, same sleepless nights. A few years ago, someone wrote a book called *The Secret Footballer*. While it was absolutely no secret in the game who the player behind the mask was, I get why he wanted to shield his identity. There's a temptation when you're still in football not to talk openly about the deeper, maybe even darker, aspects of the game. You're not meant to do stuff like that. Find yourself in front of a reporter or TV camera and it's supposed to be all 'we're happy with the three points' or 'we'll move on to the next game to put things right'. Football's not a game where anyone is encouraged to talk freely. Clubs don't want you to do that because you might say something they don't like. The people who run a sport worth billions are a lot happier if there's an impression that everything is as gleaming and polished as it seems to be. That's great. It works. The Premier League is an incredibly successful organisation. But football does kind of ignore the fact that the ones who make the whole thing work – the players – are real people.

I didn't want to write a book from the shadows. With a long career spanning non-league to the top division and into Europe, and having experienced the biggest highs and the most crushing of lows along the way, I knew I was better placed than anyone to reveal what the life of a footballer is really like. I knew also that, having accessed therapy, having embraced that idea of really understanding myself and my emotions, I could talk about the game and its impact, good and bad, in a more detailed, and hopefully informed way than maybe I could have a few years ago. People say there's only one certainty in football – that nothing's certain. And life's the same. So, if you're going to be a footballer you have to deal with the fact that those two things are going to rub up against each other every now and then. I don't think it hurts to say that out loud. In fact, I think exactly the opposite. The more honest we are about ourselves as footballers, the easier it is to live our lives.

And that applies to everyone. I've written a book about football, but what I hope more than anything is that a lot of what I've spoken about will click with people, no matter who they are. You don't have to be a footballer to find yourself lying in bed one day wondering whether you can face carrying on in the same way as before. That can happen to anyone. The point I'm making is there are ways of dealing with it.

Times have changed. When it comes to mental health, in the last few years especially, we're looking at a different world. It's OK for men to go and talk to someone, to ask for help. In fact, I can guarantee you'll be happy that you've done so. I've been asked many times why I'm writing this book and that, more than anything, is the number one reason. If a single person feeling bad about themselves or their life is inspired by my story to go and talk to someone then it's been worth every one of these words. If I can do it, from a strong Jamaican culture of men not sharing their troubles in public, and from a sporting culture where for a long time 'being a man' meant, whatever your private troubles, putting on a brave face and pretending to be something you weren't, then I truly believe that anyone can do the same. If you are that person, my message is simple. Get help. It will be the best thing you ever do.

I'm more than happy to tell anyone who'll listen that therapy changed my life. I swear by it 100 per cent. I still do it now, because it sows the seeds of happiness – the most important thing in life. If you're happy, you make the people around you happy. I've always been that glass half-full person, and allowing my emotions to come to the surface has only made me more so. Since the crash I've been more emotional than ever. I suppose that's what happens when you come face to face with death. Of course, there's a rawness to that experience – it's something I wouldn't wish on anyone – but at the same time I've enjoyed being more sensitive because it's helped me release a lot of the stuff in my head that before I'd have forced back down. I've come to see my life as a total rollercoaster, but one that I'd never change, because with every up and every down I've learned so much. I'll carry those lessons with me wherever I go. I live a hectic life – football, family, punditry, business – and have to make sure I'm looking after my mental and physical health along the way.

I think I'll be remembered as a footballer who always tried to enjoy himself; a happy boy, someone who tried his hardest, who played with a smile on his face, made the most of any bad situations and who just enjoyed his job. But wherever I've been on my rollercoaster ride, one thing has never changed – my faith in making things happen for myself. I never stopped believing that I'd make it as a footballer, that I'd play at the very highest level. Maybe I'd even win something! Which I did. You might remember this book started with me gripped by the kind of stress and mental overload that hits us all at certain times. It just so happened to hit me straight after the biggest game of my life. I'm so happy I was eventually able to enjoy the magnitude of that achievement. So many players go through their careers without winning anything. But I did, and no-one can ever take that away from me. Seeing all those West Ham fans celebrating on the open-top bus parade was amazing. A reminder of what football means to us all. The absolute joy it can bring – often because so much pain has come before.

I was 33 when I finally got my hands on that trophy. I've definitely had longevity of career. I'll be honest, there's perhaps bits of it I didn't expect when I started out. I never thought I'd end up as West Ham's highest Premier League goalscorer. I'm also not ready to give up my football just yet.

I want my time in the game to end on a high, at the very least to bow out on my own terms rather than lying in the wreckage of a Ferrari.

It's not something I particularly want to think about, but had the worst happened that day, I expect all the reaction would have been based around me as a footballer. Games played, goals scored, etc. Then at the bottom of the newspaper article would have been a couple of paragraphs about me as a person. I hope this book will go some way to changing that; to encouraging an understanding that we're people first and footballers second. Sons, brothers and fathers as well as defenders, midfielders and strikers. We wear a kit, but we have our own skin. We are, at our core, just like anyone else. The rest of the game might change. The stadiums might get larger, the TV coverage bigger, the transfer fees more out of this world. But we, the players, never will.

Humans, not robots. That's us. And it will be that way forever.

POSTSCRIPT

March 2026

I was determined my footballing career wouldn't end with a car crash. Now I can look myself in the mirror and say, hand on heart, I made that promise come true.

As the spring of 2026 came round, I was training with Charlton Athletic. Everything was going well and they were on the verge of offering me a contract until the end of the season. That's when I got a phone call from my Jamaica teammate Mason Holgate, who was playing for Al-Sailiya in Qatar. 'Our striker's just been injured. We're in a relegation scrap. Do you fancy coming out here?'

The money they were offering wasn't great, about half of what Charlton were proposing, and, let's be honest, the life-style and money are usually what persuade players to make such a move. So my first thought was, *What's the point? Why would I leave my kids behind for a deal that isn't even that good?* At first, I didn't even bother calling my agent, but when I did he thought I should at least hear them out. Have a conversation. Subsequently, Al-Sailiya invited me out to see what they were about for myself. 'If you like it, we can talk properly. If not, no harm done.'

Once I was there I could see the appeal. The weather's great, the lifestyle's relaxed, there are plenty of good restaurants, lots of expats, and everyone speaks English, so settling in isn't an issue. I really liked it.

The football side worked too. At that point in the season there were only seven games left, one a week, and for me, returning from injury, that felt perfect. A chance to ease myself back in, get minutes under my belt, and, the manager promised, build up to playing a full 90 minutes. At Charlton, on the other hand, I could be playing twice a week, high intensity, fast pace – that is if I got on the pitch. Qatar felt like a much more controlled way back. Physically and mentally, it was the perfect reintroduction to football. I could then come home and reassess my position in the summer.

I signed the contract. The first game coming up on the Saturday felt like a massive moment. I'd got so near to signing at Brentford and Leicester, but now I'd actually made it all the way.

And then the war broke out.

What is this? This can't be real. Fifteen months of working to get back, to finally be in a position to play again, and then a war? Iran against Israel and the USA? You couldn't make it up.

Early on, the club were insisting the game would go ahead. But a lot of the lads weren't comfortable. I understood that, but at the same time I was thinking, *It's taken me 15 months to get here. I'm playing!* Some of the local players felt the same – they were ready to go. In the end, though, the game was called off. It was the right decision. No matter how much you want to play, no matter how long you've waited, you don't want to be stepping on to a pitch in the middle of a war zone. And as it turned out, that Saturday night – the night the game was meant to be played – was when everything really kicked off.

I was in my hotel room when I started hearing it – *Bang! Bang! Bang!* Missiles, distant but unmistakable. At first I tried to ignore the noise, but it kept going. I went over to the window and looked out. I couldn't see the missiles themselves, not clearly, but I could see the red trail behind them cutting across the sky. I must have seen 20 of them, all moving in the same direction, streaking across to my right. And then, seconds later – impact! The whole hotel was starting to shake. You could feel the vibration through the walls, through the floor. It was surreal. *This is insane!* The missiles were landing maybe 20 miles away – but it didn't matter. It felt close. I genuinely thought, *Is this a sign?* Like something bigger than me was trying to tell me something. Like God was saying, *Michail, this isn't where you're meant to be.*

Over the next few days the club were trying to get us back in to train, at a facility only about 10 minutes from a military barracks. That changed everything for me. Being out there to play football is one thing, but going to train right next to a potential target – that's a completely different situation. I just thought, *No. I'm not doing that.* A few of the lads felt the same, so for a couple of days some of us didn't turn up for training. It wasn't about being difficult. It was about basic safety.

The Qatar Stars League arranged a Zoom call with the players. They were trying to reassure everyone. 'Your safety is our top priority. We'll do everything we can to make it safe and get the games on.' But they were also honest. They said if things continued the way they were, there was a real chance the games wouldn't go ahead at all.

While the attack I'd heard from the hotel was frightening, I'm glad to say Qatar is generally a very safe place. There are strong defence systems in place, and most missiles and drones were being intercepted before they could cause any damage. I never actually saw a missile hit anything myself. But you could hear the interceptions, the distant impacts. That was the thing, the sound. No matter how safe a place is meant to be, when you're hearing explosions it changes how you think.

When I heard reports that an Iranian cell had entered Qatar, that was it for me. *Right, I'm going home.* Around the same time, the next game got called off anyway. So I packed my things and the plan was to be driven from Qatar to Riyadh in Saudi Arabia. That's a journey that ordinarily should take four hours but in the end took 12 hours and involved passing through seven different stop checks. It was a nerve-racking ordeal. I flew back to England from there. I was home for about five days. Then the club called – the following game was going ahead. 'We need you back.' I couldn't get a direct route sorted in time, so it meant another long journey through Saudi, then into Qatar.

I flew in on the Tuesday, trained on the Wednesday and played on the Thursday. The preparation wasn't ideal, far from it, but honestly, I was buzzing just to be back out there. We lost 4–0, which was frustrating, but at the same time there was something bigger going on. After everything – the injuries, the setbacks, the uncertainty – I'd made it back on to the pitch for 73 minutes. That mattered. Of course, part of me always imagined that my last game would be in the Premier League. But the reality was I'd played again. I'd officially stepped back on to a pitch in a club game.

That means everything. The crash isn't the final chapter of my football story. It's not how it ends.

Looking forward, Qatar feels like the right place for me to be. That doesn't mean I've written off coming back to England or playing at a higher level again. Not at all. It just means, for this moment, this is what's best for me, and if that means I'm here for a couple of years, then great. Being here just makes sense. When I nearly signed for Brentford, that was 10 months after the crash. Leicester City was 12 months. Now it's 15 months, and the difference in my body is night and day. At Brentford, even getting through training meant needing deep massage treatment just to get my leg ready. Now I can train without any massage at all if I want to. My mobility, my movement, everything feels like it's back to where it was before the crash. Qatar is a good environment to rebuild and reset, and right now that's exactly what I'm doing.

At the same time, it's undeniably weird. As I'm writing this, a warning alert is going off on my phone.

That sound means a missile or drone has entered Qatari airspace. That's the thing – you can be sitting there, relaxing, trying to switch off, and then suddenly your phone lights up, the alarm goes off, and everything changes in an instant. In the middle of the night you're jumping up out of bed, heart racing. *What's happening now?* There's that split second of panic every time. And then sometimes, a few moments later, you hear a distant bang.

As I write this I can't help but reflect on the dreadful toll this war is taking on the people in the wider region and the horrifying loss of human life, as well as the damaging impact on people's livelihoods and their emotional and mental health. It puts everything into perspective.

But the war won't last forever. Things will settle. And when they do, Qatar is a great place to be. The lifestyle, the facilities, the way of life. There are far worse places you could spend a few years.

In the meantime, for me it's about focusing on the football, getting those minutes, and proving – to everyone else, but also to myself – that I'm back. Hopefully this is my chance to show people that I can still play. That's why, for me, this has been the right decision. Not just for now, but for whatever comes next in my career.

It all depends on the opportunities. What comes up, what feels right. But today, all I know is I'm a footballer. And I'm happy.

ACKNOWLEDGEMENTS

I would like to thank the following people:

John Antonio – you've been massive for me. Best friend, mentor, brother.

Mike Appiason – much more than my agent. So close to me that I see you as another brother.

Mum – you were the person who always believed in me; always pushed me to do anything that made me happy. Dad, you were the rock of the family. And, like Mum, always just wanted me to be happy.

Nigel Gibbs – you saw me arrive in professional football from non-league. There was so much missing at that stage. You could have so easily bypassed me. Instead, you went out of your way, gave me your time and helped.

Stuart Gray – you didn't coach me for long at Sheffield Wednesday, but you pushed me to better myself. You gave me the opportunity to take that next step up and show my class at a higher level.

Dave Sullivan – you didn't have to, but you took the gamble on me and introduced me to the Premier League. At West Ham you believed in me and repeatedly gave me contracts.

Marlon Fleischmann and Will Salthouse – two great agents who have played such an incredibly supportive role in my career, pushing me in the right direction.

David Moyes – thank you for helping me become a European champion.

Thanks also to John Woodhouse for his help writing this book, to Sam Bailey and Darryl Duah-Boateng, and to Jonathan Taylor and all at HarperCollins for making it possible.